Divine Anarchy:

The Writings

CJ Story

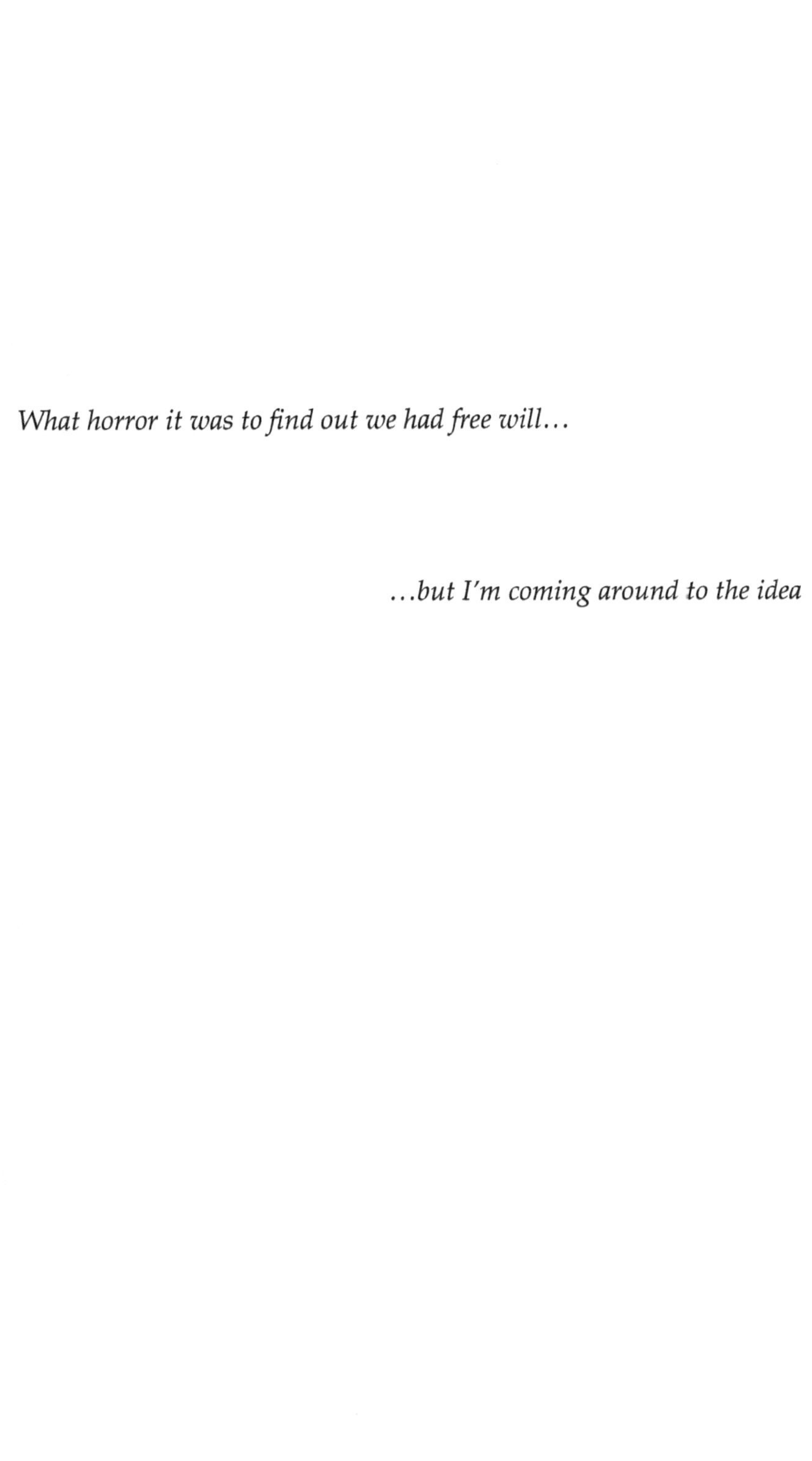

What horror it was to find out we had free will…

…but I'm coming around to the idea

CONTENTS

Lights In The Jungle - Rainy months 1489BC

In the year before years, when the rivers cut through the Supe Valley and the bones of the Caral rose in step-pyramids against the sand, a man walked into the jungle. He was a leader among his people though there was no crown sitting on his head, no iron sword at his side - this was the time before iron. It was a time when Man didn't rule by conquest or war but by trade. Music existed, played on the bone flute around fires that burned in the plaza pits. The man's name would never be written or kept, no glyphs survived his people, only knots in cords. Strings of cords, strings of quipu swaying in the dark.

Beyond the huts, the man's bare feet stepped through the dirt of the jungle. The night was a great animal, its breathing was the chorus of insects, its eyes were the moon and the stars but then there were lights that were neither the moon nor the stars.

He saw them first as glimmerings in the distance, faint and flickering like embers. They didn't move like torches or fireflies but with an apparent purpose unknown to Man. They came and went among the boles of the ceiba trees, sometimes low to the ground, other times rising up to the stars. The man thought of rival tribes. He thought of enemies. He thought of Gods and the blood in his fingers grew cold.

The knotted cord he carried was made by his forefathers to count the harvests, to tie together the seasons, to recall the days when the solstice sun fell square on the plazas. He ran it through his trembling hands as he walked.

It was the rainy months but it was dry. There was no wind moving the leaves. He took position behind a tree and watched the lights dance. One of the lights zipped up, vertical towards the Heavens faster than the eye could track, before zipping back and settling again among the trees.

The man knelt, not in worship, but in exhaustion like a beast hit by an arrow. When he bent his head the lights came closer and the beat of his heart sped up. He thought of sacrifices, of the flames that his people fed in the temple pits.

The earth around him began to glow and the lights swirled directly above him, circling, dancing and following one another as if now part of one singular object.

The man raised his head skywards, the lights illuminating his face like sunlight.

With eyes closed against the light he saw all things happening at the same time. Behind all the things happening all at once, he saw there was no reason and no order but pure anarchy .

There was an explosion of light and rock and nothing for the longest of times, and then finally there was life that the man could recognise as life, fish that could be recognised as fish, then there were beasts like no beasts he had ever seen walking and flying through a Earth that had no Humans, then stars falling and burning, then there were new oceans, then new rivers and mountains, then apes, soon after there were cities with vast steel and glass structures tearing into the sky, giant winged machines flying, Man looking at Earth whilst standing on the ground of the Moon, millions - no - billions of Humans, chimneys with black smoke, beasts dying in deserts, oceans rising, billions becoming millions, then humans looking at the Earth on a red planet, then just ocean, no land, then millions became thousands, thousands became hundreds, finally a great silence among the universe and figures, not Human, coming from the silent void, from a dimension that was there all along but couldn't be seen, he saw them trying to communicate to the Humans who couldn't see them, they tried for millennia before they gave up and millennia later they found a way to break through but it was all too late.

Then the lights were gone. The man was left on his knees, in the darkness, his face looking up to the sky, his eyes closed. The chorus of insects had stopped.

When the man returned to his people his face was ash-pale. They asked what he had seen after he went to investigate the lights. He stood in silence for a long time, his hands raw from the cord that he still carried.

He then said,

"Nothing. There was nothing"

That night they painted the lights on stone, circles within circles, sparks etched in ochre. They played music on a flute made of deer bone and they stomped the earth and danced around a roaring fire. The man sat back from the light of the fire and looked at his people. He saw them as ghosts already. The man thought of how he was just another witness, no more, no less, existing by chance beneath an empty sky.

And long after his body became earth, men still spoke of the lights in the jungle and it was decided that it must have been divine, an intervention of the Gods - for what else is there?

The City - May 1998

 A short walk from my middle school there was an abandoned garage, like an old mechanic's shop, wedged between a parcel distribution depot on the left and a physical therapy center on the right. There was a forecourt at the front, and despite the garage showing no signs of life, its graffitied metal shutters pulled down at all times, the businesses around it stuck to their own part of the lot. The garage's section was always empty except for one long estate car from the eighties, up on bricks with no wheels.
We were encouraged to walk in groups when we left school and to look out for one another. The threat of "bad men" was always looming, and we were constantly reminded in assemblies, health classes, and random talks throughout the school day. Once, the principal went around to every class holding up a police mugshot of a man and told us to run into a store if we ever saw him and tell the store owner.

So, four eleven-year-olds set off walking home together at 3 p.m. after the final school bell rang. Four eleven-year-olds versus the countless bad men we were told were out there in the city, just waiting.

In winter, it would start getting dark by two-thirty, and most of my memories of walking home were in the dark, which strangely felt safer in many ways. It was easier to go unnoticed in the dark. It was easier to see the well-lit areas and stay away from the darker ones. But now, in the spring 3 p.m. sunshine, there was no hiding. The areas that were "dark no-go" zones in winter were now masquerading, camouflaged in the light.

We reached the abandoned garage and decided, for no reason, to try to get inside. The shutters were locked. One of us kicked it, and from the back of the estate car, a rough voice shouted, "Stop that, you little bastards!"

It was a homeless guy. He looked old, had wiry gray stubble, and about three teeth. He stank of piss and booze.

We laughed at him. One of us asked, "Is that your house?" and we laughed even harder.

He wasn't making any sense but was getting angrier, shifting himself along the backseat of the car, struggling to stay upright and open the door.

We kept laughing and walked just far enough away to run if needed, but not far enough to stop the fun we were having tormenting the guy. One of us picked up a stone and threw it at the car.

He swore and shouted, mumbling and groaning. He'd gotten the door open and swung one leg out — his foot wrapped in newspaper.

We threw another stone, and it hit him in the face. He shuffled in the seat, and despite making no attempt to get out, we told ourselves he was about to chase us. We ran away screaming and laughing, convincing one another that we'd escaped him.

The city, we'd been told, was full of bad men.

Around this time, I had my first girlfriend — or as much of a
girlfriend as an eleven-year-old can have. She was super pretty,
warm, and funny. I couldn't believe she wanted to sit next to me in
class, that she spoke to me at recess. When my friends made fun of
me for being in love, I was embarrassed, but at the same time, proud
that this girl liked me.

One day, we left school together, just me and her, walking side by
side. She said, *"Hold my hand."* It was an order, not an invitation. I
held her hand and my heart exploded. I had the kind of butterflies
you can only feel when you're eleven years old.

We reached the abandoned garage, and the homeless guy was
standing outside the car this time. Over the months, he'd added
more and more of his possessions — mostly trash bags and boxes —
inside the car and around it.

He was rooting through one of the bags as we walked by, hand in
hand. He looked up at me, recognizing me as one of the kids who'd
thrown stones at his car before running away. On my way home, I'd
shouted names at him from afar.

We watched one another as I passed by. In my mind, I was pleading
for him not to confront me. Not now, not when everything was
perfect and I was holding hands with a girl I was pretty sure I loved.

He didn't.

We kept walking into the center of the city that was forever busy,
with lines of buses constantly pulling in and setting off, and the

occasional siren breaking through the hum of traffic and voices. It was along a row of shops that we saw him — the guy from the mugshot the principal had shown us. He looked skinnier than in the picture, with sores and blisters across his face. He was swaying more than walking, people parting around him, avoiding eye contact. His eyes locked onto mine and he grinned wide, showing brown, crooked teeth.

"That's that guy," my girlfriend said.

We didn't walk anywhere near him. We changed direction. She told me the sensible thing to do was what the principal had told us — go into a store and tell someone.

The store we went into was a secondhand VHS, cassette, and vinyl shop.

We walked to the counter, where a middle-aged, fat man stood reading a newspaper. My girlfriend nudged me forward to speak with him. He looked down at me.

I told him, "There's a bad man outside — the one the school warned us about. We're supposed to tell someone if we see him."

The man glanced at the window, then back at me.

"Get the fuck out of here, kid."

Constant - May 2001

Back when I was thirteen, there was this guy at the skate park who
called himself Constant.

As kids, we never questioned it — never considered it wasn't his real
name, or that he had simply decided one day that was who he was
and never looked back.

He told us he was half Vietnamese. He had a long, sun-bleached
beard that reached his chest and a tan you only get from living
around salt and sand. His hair jutted out in every direction and
formed a halo around the top of his head. He used to hang out on the
edge of the park with a joint burning between his fingers.

He never let us kids hit it when we asked.
He'd wave us off with a grin, saying,
"Nah, y'all young'uns gotta stay focused."

Sometimes he walked around barefoot, other times in worn leather
sandals — always in baggy linen trousers and faded T-shirts. He'd
usually have a book in his hand, a different one every time.

Adults didn't like him. They said he was a bum, or a weirdo. We
were told not to talk to him. But we loved him. He was one of us — a
grown-up who'd escaped growing up. He drifted between the skate
park and the beach, talking with whoever stopped: buskers, tourists,
locals walking dogs.

At sunset, Venice Beach came alive — crowds gathering to watch the
sun drop behind the mountains — and Constant would appear,

carrying a giant tote bag full of steaming foil trays. He said he spent his days batch-cooking in his little kitchen: rice and beans, noodles, roasted chicken falling apart in sauce. He handed the meals out like communion to whoever was hungry — homeless guys, kids, old men who'd drunk their money away.

There was never any judgment, never a question. No *"Do you want this?"* or *"Can I give this to you?"* He'd press a tray into a set of hands like it wasn't charity but friendship.

The most he ever said when handing food over was:
"Here."
"I made extra, man."
Or simply, "I made this for you."

It was rare to see him sitting. He was rail-thin, and sometimes people said he looked like he was tweaking — always moving, even when he was standing still. I never thought he did anything stronger than weed. I figured he was just restless, like the current beneath the tide.

Which was strange, because his whole aura was calm — like he understood the universe in a way the rest of us didn't yet, and he was patient enough to wait while we caught up.

When Constant spoke to you directly, it felt like being chosen. The first time he spoke to me, I'd come off my board, palms grazed, pride bruised. I'd thrown my deck down the park in frustration, watched it bounce off the concrete and slide across the path. Constant walked over, picked it up, brushed the dust from the grip tape, and handed it back.

"Pain's just proof you're tryin'," he said, smiling.

One minute he'd be clapping and whooping when one of us landed
an ollie, and the next we'd be crowded around him, listening to him
talk about galaxies, energy, and how space was still expanding.

He said there was no such thing as time. That we were the ones
who'd save the world — because we could choose to be either heroes
or villains, and it was our job to choose right. He talked about
positive and negative forces, the yin and yang of everything, and
how we had to tip the scales toward good.

"You guys are heroes, right? You're all good guys here, yeah?"

Yeah, we'd say in unison.

He'd describe how sound could make sand form into perfect
patterns — cymatics, he called it — the proof that even chaos carried
beauty.

"That's creation," he'd say. "That's the universe showing off. You put
good things out, you get good things back."

He told us we were all made of stardust.
That we were part of everything.
And we had no reason not to believe him or take it as absolute fact.

I remember once a fight broke out between a couple of kids about a
year or so older than me at the skate park. One of them had a
bloodied nose, the other a torn shirt. After it had all died down —
the shouting, the kids grouping around — Constant sat on one of the

ramps, legs dangling, smoke from his joint curling around him.

He shook his head at the two guys who had been fighting and said
calmly to them,
"There's power in mercy."

As the sun dipped and the meals had all been handed out, Constant
would be on the beach with a CD player, cheap wired headphones
trailing down his shirt to his pocket. He'd dance with whoever
wanted to join — this strange man with a long, thin beard stepping
side to side, shaking one leg, then the other, raising his hands,
blasting Fleetwood Mac.

Tourists were usually the brave ones. They'd dance with him as their
shyer friends laughed and took photos. Constant never cared. He
was happy if he had someone to dance with. He was happy if he
didn't.

Like vampires only come out in the dark and return to their crypt at
dawn, Constant only appeared at golden hour and disappeared by
the time it was fully dark. He never said goodbye — just drifted
away when the air cooled and the boardwalk emptied. Occasionally
he stayed longer, and we felt like we'd been given a gift.

One evening, he didn't appear at golden hour.
Homeless guys waited around, hands empty. We skated until dark.
There was no Constant the next day, or the next.

We never saw him again.

I always figured that Constant already had peace — never that he was searching for it. It was like he understood everything. Like he knew the answers to the universe but kept them to himself, waiting for the rest of us to catch up.

He wasn't trying to reach nirvana; he was already in it.

Nirvana was that golden hour each night, on that beach — sharing. Sharing food, sharing wisdom, sharing music, sharing the sunset with everyone. Sharing the boulevard with the magicians, blues players, violinists, little kids firing bubble guns, listening to problems, providing advice in the context of our existence among the stars.

He taught me that reaching nirvana is easy — it's simply a state of mind. It's not gained through striving and trying. Sure, you should strive and try in life, but to be peaceful — to be truly peaceful — you need to practice it by just doing.

Doing it barefoot, in motion. Feeding the hungry. Reading. Educating yourself and others. Dancing in the last golden light of the day.

That was Constant.

The Mentor - November 2008

Shouts, laughter, cheering.

The streets were crowded with thousands, though it was long past midnight and I was knee-deep in a freezing water fountain with my jeans rolled up. I kicked water at a group of strangers who screamed and splashed back. Firecrackers snapped through Washington Square. A red flare hissed on the path, smoke lifting into the cold night.

Obama had just been named President. For the first time in my twenty-one years there was hope — bright and reckless — a kind of optimism my generation had never touched and, as it turned out, wouldn't again for decades.

That night I met Luca.

I never asked his age, but I guessed sixties. He was a big man — tall, broad, with a mane of gray hair and beard. Sunglasses clung to the end of his nose — sunglasses past midnight. He passed me a joint with the ease of an old friend. Amid the noise and jubilation, fireworks and megaphones, we smoked and spoke of politics, of hope, of art. We learned we were both painters. I told him I wrote.

I took a long drag, blew it out into the night —

— and the ocean was sweeping stones against the shore. Birds sang from the jungle, crickets in chorus. February 2009, a week before my twenty-second birthday. I had flown to Puerto Rico during a university break. Luca had come down from New York to meet me at a commune.

There were maybe a dozen of us: two French girls my age, a handful of middle-aged solo travelers, pairs in their twenties and thirties. Four musicians, two writers, the rest artists. Luca was the oldest; I was the youngest.

"Heyyyyyy maaaaan…" he said, in the same stretched cadence I'd loved in Washington Square. We hadn't met since November, but we'd stayed in touch. The internet — still new to me — had made it possible. Luca was a New Yorker, born to Polish immigrants, but travel had softened his edges. He carried himself with a West Coast breeziness.

When we met at the airport, he wore a soft cardigan, a hefty rucksack on his back, a faded Creedence T-shirt with heavy black glasses hanging from the neck, shorts, old boots with black socks. On his face — the same sunglasses from November.

The point of the commune was simple: to breathe, to strip away the grind, to make something free of routine and noise. I painted on the beach in pajama bottoms, the sun glaring white.

"What do you want?" Luca asked me one of those days. "What do you want from this art stuff?"
"I dunno. I guess for people to like it."
He laughed.
"Well, look… for a start, there's no good art, no bad art. Hell, there's nothing even original anymore. The rest — people liking it, not

liking it, time, judgment, the outside world — all of that stuff is an illusion, right? What you should want is for your art to let you stay outside that illusion, open to that place where you create. Art lets you lean into it. And when you're there… you're there in the purest place. That's something out of this world, man. Beyond our understanding. It's creation! It's divine! Everything was born from it, and we'll all meet there again in the end!"

He laughed again, and I said nothing.

The sky stretched above us like an endless canvas.

Luca's words never really needed a reply. You just let them sit with you, considering them. Sometimes they sounded like nonsense — like when he told us about reptilians — but sometimes they were profound. His kindness, his wisdom, his humor, his joy — they pulled people in.

The nights we spent with the other travelers in the commune — taking turns cooking, sitting around beach fires, laughing, getting high, running half-naked into the sea at sunset — those moments, however small, I realized, were all moments like the ones he was talking about. Divinity. Not planned, not forced. Beyond explanation, just fleeting instants occurring in the cosmos. They meant nothing and everything all at once.

I squinted through the light and kept painting.

On the last morning of the trip, I woke to a silence in the commune that didn't feel right. Nobody could find Luca. I went down to the beach to see if he'd gotten up early and gone swimming.

He had — only when I got there, I found him lying face-down in the sand, the ocean washing around him.

Later we learned it was a heart attack. He had died instantly. They told us he was sixty-four.

That was Luca — the man who first introduced me to divinity.

Ionian Astronauts - July 2010

There was an old story that Cleopatra, caught in a storm, sought refuge on an Ionian island. Back then it was covered in olive trees, the air heavy with wild herbs, the turquoise ocean crashing against rugged coastlines.

In 2010, it was still covered in olive trees, still smelled of wild herbs, and the same turquoise ocean still crashed into its rugged coastlines. Only now there wasn't Cleopatra on the beach staring out across the water, but me, lying in a hammock in the shade of an olive grove, watching planes dip toward Corfu.

There was a line in a song by The National — *nobody knows where you are* — and that was exactly how I felt when I was on the island. Tourism hadn't really taken off back then. Villas were few and far between, nothing like the explosion a decade later. There was only one hotel.

Back then, I had to reach the island by flying into Corfu and catching a ride with a fisherman and his wife, who trundled their boat across the Ionian Sea in pitch darkness, stars blazing above us. It took over an hour. We had to climb up the harbor wall from the boat, but it beat waiting twelve hours for the passenger ferry — a service so unreliable that a slight breeze could cancel it.

I'd been to the island a lot. I'd spend days in a hammock, writing, swimming, taking boats to hidden coves, eating seafood, picking limes from the tree outside my door. The nights were hot, alive, full of laughter and music and people — locals and tourists (mostly from Italy) sitting in the Venetian-style squares until past midnight.

One particular night there was chatter going around the square that something had crashed just up the coast. Some thought it might be a plane or a helicopter. There was one fire truck on the north of the island — from the 1980s — that had made its way to the scene after they rounded up the firemen, who worked in a variety of bars and restaurants, to tell them there was an actual, honest-to-God emergency.

When they got there, the crash site was on a hill beside the road that wound up from the harbor. On its other side was a drop down to the ocean, and in the distance, the mountains on the mainland.

The crashed object was unmistakably an Apollo capsule — cone-shaped, scorched, a Russian flag on its side. It leaned to one side, lodged in the earth at the end of the violent, burning trail it had carved. The bottom was scorched from white heat, and two giant parachutes trailed into the sea below.

The firemen were dressed in jeans and shorts — one even in chef whites. They turned on their hose and put out the fires.

The hatch split open with a hiss of old air. An astronaut stepped out into the Greek night in his white suit, helmet under his arm. There was no podium, no ticker tape — only three Greek firemen who gave him an inquiring *"You good?"*thumbs-up. The astronaut gave a thumbs-up back.

One fireman pointed him toward the one town on the south of the island. Another stopped a passing pickup truck driven by an old man and chatted away in Greek. A few minutes later, the astronaut was sitting in the back of the truck, being driven into town.

I saw him that first night after the crash. When he climbed out of the pickup and walked into the square, the straps of his suit hung loose and he had his gloves tucked under his arm. He cradled his helmet like a priceless object. Some children stared at him wide-eyed while gripping their grandmothers' hands. Mostly, nobody looked at all.

He took a seat outside one of the bars and just sat, watching, waiting for it all to make sense. He didn't order, but someone brought him a beer and a gyro.

He sipped the beer and ate the food — which, I figured, was better than recycled water and tablets of protein he'd been living on. As the night went on, his face softened. After midnight, as always, the crowd thinned to bar staff sweeping, stacking chairs, and eventually the astronaut was alone.

For the next couple of days, children would run up to him shouting "Astronaftis!" and dare each other to say hello. But by the third day, they'd grown bored of him. He moved from the square — where he'd been sleeping and eating free food from kind strangers — to the harbor wall, where he sat looking out at the ocean.

He stopped a local and tapped a picture of the ferry that hadn't run in a week. The local shrugged and walked on. At night, he walked the shoreline with his head tilted up to the constellations — the same ones he'd been living among, though they seemed more distant now.

He knelt in the sand and used a stick to draw orbital paths and formulas, but the sea erased them by dawn. He spoke Russian, I think, but it didn't matter. Whoever he spoke to just shrugged and carried on.

I didn't see him again for a week, and by that point, he'd been letting the suit go. He bartered the gloves first for fruit. I don't know who got them, but I saw one glove later on a wall by the road, tangled in vines.

The helmet went next. For a while, it sat behind a bar. Then the children claimed it, running through alleys with it balanced on their heads. He cut the torso of the suit into a vest eventually.

Another week went by, and I flew home to the UK. I didn't return to the island until the end of summer.

When I went past the crash site, the earth looked normal again, but the capsule was rusting badly. To my surprise, the astronaut was sitting cross-legged on the opposite side of the road in the shade. He looked like everyone else — shorts, sandals, a T-shirt with an American logo. His hair was longer now, bleached by the sun, his skin deeply tanned. He stared at the rusting capsule, still leaning to one side, its parachutes long gone.

Eventually, people stopped calling it the Apollo and started saying it was just an old buoy abandoned decades ago.

The story changed every time I told it. In one version, he never removed the suit. He walked the island forever sealed inside, an anonymous visitor. In another, he vanished into the sea one night, helmet back on. In yet another, he married a woman from the island and had children who grew up hearing bedtime stories of zero gravity — of the Earth rising like a marble over the moon's edge.

No one believes any version of the story, of course.

I walked past that capsule one last time before I left. The sea was flat, the cicadas loud. I stopped and touched the rust. It was warm under my hand, flaking, but solid. I half expected to hear echoes inside — a hollow voice counting down, the beeps of a control panel, the roar of it burning up.

Nothing. Just the sound of soft waves.

I still think of that island most days — its beauty, the fish in the pristine water, the laid-back locals, the cicadas all night and all day, the silence when the generator cut out and the whole island paused.

And I think of the astronaut — alone or not alone — walking under those same stars I see now.

Twenty Mirrors in SoHo, London
- October 2012

The corridor to the toilets was lined with mirrors, and I couldn't tell which one was the door. Purple LEDs ran along the floor like an airport runway for the lost.

I pressed one mirror — it flexed but didn't open. My own sweating face stared back, too close, too alive. I turned to another, then another. Twenty of me turned too, each trying to escape. Was that my reflection, or was I his? My heart was kicking against my ribs. I started pressing mirrors faster, palms slipping, breath snagging on the bass leaking through the walls.

The corridor began to sway, left then right, as if the building itself was dancing. The beat thudded in my jaw, in my teeth, in the small bones of my ears.

Behind me, a mirror opened and two men stepped out. Their eyes caught the purple light — pupils wide, whites glowing. They brushed past, glaring down at me, before moving like ghosts through the dark.

I lunged for the mirror they came through. My reflection lunged back. When our fingertips met, the glass folded inward and light spilled out like revelation. The restroom.

I stumbled inside, slammed a cubicle door, locked it.

The rush hit like a train.

Every sound was too loud — the fluorescent hum, the hiss of pipes, the static inside my skull. My heartbeat was an earthquake trapped in my chest. My shirt clung to me; sweat soaked the waistband of my jeans. My mouth was dry, but my jaw wouldn't stop moving, grinding at nothing. My hands shook so hard I pressed them to the walls just to feel something solid.

I was vibrating — every nerve lit, every thought electric and useless. The room breathed with me, faster, faster.

I didn't want to die like this. Not in London. Not in a toilet.

Hours later, I was on the train home. The fields slid past in ribbons of silver and gold. My friends were asleep — mouths open, heads rocking with the rhythm of the tracks. I sat there in that strange calm after the storm — heart finally slowing, body hollowed out but mind still spinning.

The night was over, the day hadn't begun. And in the faint reflection on the window, I could still see that corridor — the twenty versions of me, still sweating, still pushing at glass, each of them convinced they were the one who'd find the way out.

The Vermilion Man - September 2014

The TV in the corner of the emergency room was showing an ice cap breaking off and falling into the sea.

It was some documentary, maybe. Or a news show. Something about polar bears stranded on ice, with sweeping helicopter shots of a vast, cold ocean.

In the reflection of the screen was Sirius's face — long, solemn. He watched the screen unblinking, standing in the middle of dozens of empty plastic chairs in the artificially bright space. A clock ticked on the wall. An empty fold-up wheelchair sat to the side.

Patients would have filled the room some hours ago, and in a few hours they would fill it again — with illness, broken bones, torn ligaments, wounds, and coughing children.

Now there were penguins.
Penguins covered in snow, sitting on eggs.

"Mr. Parker?"
Sirius turned to the nurse.
"Mr. Parker, you can come back through to the family room now."

There were great sheets of ice in the ocean, a soaking-wet polar bear leaping back into the water.

"Why is it so quiet in here?" Sirius asked in a barely audible murmur.
"Excuse me, Mr. Parker?"

"I said, why is it so quiet in here? I thought emergency rooms were always busy."

"Well, uh, sometimes they can be, Mr. Parker. Tonight's a quiet night, I guess. The daytime's very busy, though."

"How's that?"

"How's what?"

"How is it that it can be busy at four p.m. but so quiet at four a.m.? If people are ill, they're ill, right? It's pretty convenient they only get ill in daylight hours."

"Well, I guess people are more active — there are more injuries, maybe."

Sirius nodded.

There was an icy-blue crevice as high as the Statue of Liberty, right down the side of a glacier. Parts of it broke and fell silently.

"We can see about getting you those stitches too, Mr. Parker."

Sirius turned to see the nurse holding her arm out to him like he was a feral animal that might bite. He watched her arm slowly link around his, and then he was moving with her across the room, over the buffered floor, through another bright — too bright — corridor.

The corridor was empty apart from a doctor in scrubs at the far end, standing beside an open door off to the side.

More ice fell on the unwatched television. Waves crashed into the glacier. There was a penguin's eye now, staring through the snow.

Step by step, Sirius and the nurse reached the doctor, whose expression didn't change. He gestured with his hand to the open door, and they moved through it.

Smoke chimneys now. Industrial factories. Cities. An Asian country full of commuters wearing face masks.

Sirius sat on one of the two sofas in the room. There was no other furniture except a coffee table, but it was screwed to the floor — less to throw, less to break.

A painting hung above one of the sofas, the frame screwed to the wall. It was a landscape — a cornfield at dusk, a farmhouse in the distance with a light on in an upstairs window.

The doctor closed the door and sat on the other sofa. The nurse sat beside Sirius and gripped his hand.

The doctor spoke, but to Sirius his voice sounded distant.
"Mr. Parker, I'm so very sorry, but I have some extremely difficult news to share with you."

There were people waist-deep in water now, carrying their children above their heads, wading forward in great numbers. Cars submerged to their roofs.

"Despite our best efforts, the injuries to your wife and daughter were ultimately too great, and they have not survived."

There were fires now — firefighters in silver suits beating at dry grass, surrounded by smoke.

Sirius touched his head and felt the open gash above his eye.
He nodded.

"Is there someone we can call for you?" the nurse asked.
"I, uh… I need to call Lisa's mom. My mother-in-law. She lives in
Florida. I don't want to wake her, though. Can I… can I see them?"

The doctor looked at the nurse, who gripped Sirius's hand tighter.
"Of course you can," the doctor said and rose to his feet. "They're in
the same cubicle. They're together."

Sirius and the nurse stood and followed the doctor out of the room.
The smell of antiseptic grew stronger. There were more sounds now
— beeping, inaudible words coming through a tannoy.

There was a row of cubicles, each one curtained in blue. Somehow
Sirius knew which one they were going to. It had a different aura
from the others — something about it that was inviting and, at the
same time, screaming for him to stay away.

The doctor pulled the curtain, and the three of them stepped inside.

There was an elephant skull now. Dust blowing across a cracked, dry
desert littered with the carcasses of dead trees.

His wife looked like she was sleeping. She was pale; her lips were
slightly blue. Her hair was scraped back, and the sheet was pulled
up to her neck. She had dried blood on her face.

His daughter lay in the next bed. Her small body was under a sheet
pulled up to her chin. She had less blood on her face. She still looked

as much like her mom as ever, but she didn't look asleep. Her eyes were closed, but her face looked trapped, uncomfortable.

Sirius touched her hair and ran it between two fingers.

Booster rockets broke away from a capsule above the curvature of the Earth and fell into space.

Sirius was back in the family room but couldn't remember leaving the cubicle. The nurse sat him on the sofa and said something about coffee, then left. The doctor was gone.

Sirius looked up at the painting of the cornfield and the house with the light on. It was a print. He guessed the hospital probably bought it for thirty dollars or so. There was no artist's signature.

In the dusk sky above the house, Sirius thought one of the clouds had the shape of an angel and a trumpet. The other clouds were just soft brushes of white paint, but this one was fuller, more defined. He stared harder and made out an eye, maybe. An elbow.

He stood up and walked out of the room.

The corridor was still empty.
To the left was the antiseptic, the beeping, the blue curtains.

He turned right and kept moving past closed doors until he was back in the ER waiting room. There was one old man now sitting on the last plastic chair in a row. He was hunched over, a deerstalker hat pulled down almost covering his eyes. A shopping trolley sat beside him, filled with plastic bags.

Sirius sat on a plastic chair at the opposite end of the room and looked back at the TV.

Protesters on the screen now — most with scarves around their faces. Flares. Great plumes of red smoke. A car in flames.

A single drop of blood from the gash on Sirius's head rolled down to the tip of his nose.

A man grabbing his child and moving to the window. He pulled back the curtain to missiles raining down, red lasers streaking into the night sky to intercept them.

The blood fell from the tip of Sirius's nose.

A police horse surged upward, standing on its hind legs. The cop on its back gripped tight as projectiles flew past him.

The blood continued to fall as Sirius remained motionless, watching the television.

A Molotov cocktail — a young woman throwing it. It smashed in front of a line of riot police with shields.

The blood hit the floor and splashed — a great explosion of red. Waves of red sloshing and crashing across the tile.

There was a protester now with a sign that read, in red paint: **"We're Entering a New Era."**

The television screen exploded and crumpled.

The wheelchair was on its side under the TV.

The old man sat bolt upright, his eyes wide.

Sirius's chair was empty.

The Gorilla - June 2014

The newspapers said the gorilla had been raised in an apartment in Florence before escaping. Others said it was part of a smuggling ring — wild animals trafficked for high-wealth clients — and it slipped free.

Either way, the gorilla lumbered down into the piazza. Some tourists ran straight away. Others stood, debating whether it was real or just a guy in a suit. Parents pointed it out to their children. Phones rose and were held toward it — photographing, videoing, live streaming.

The gorilla moved on its knuckles, its giant head swiveling, its huge brown eyes surveying the crowd beneath the Italian sun.

It wandered into a bar. Inside, it looked calm. Tourists sat with it. Some took selfies. People started feeding it peanuts, then French fries and pastries. A crowd gathered outside, pressing up against the glass, watching the gorilla eat scraps and eye anyone who crept too close for a photo.

Maybe it would have stayed that way until animal control arrived. We'll never know. We'll never know because of the Germans.

German frat boys, by all accounts. One slid a pint of beer across the floor. The gorilla picked it up and drank.

That was when it all went south. The gorilla went ape — literally.

He tore one of the Germans in half. Tables flipped. Screams broke through the bar. Blood up the walls, across the counter — blood everywhere. Outside, the crowd panicked, stampeding across the piazza in all directions.

The gorilla didn't leave the bar. That was the only mercy that day. The Italian police rolled in, blasting shots.

They hit the gorilla — and they popped a waitress by accident.

Now the place is famous. Tourists come from all over the world to line up for a drink at the hottest place in Florence:

The Gorilla Massacre Bar.

Barking At Everything, Always - August 2015

We're the sleepless dog barking at 5 a.m. in the suburban backyard.
We're the riot cop pulling on socks, hoping someone gets too close.
We're the kid getting too close and taking a baton across the ribs.
We're the bus driver letting the woman who lost her purse ride for
free.
We're the boy who would have attacked her if she wasn't let on.
We're the fisherman out at sea, bracing for storm.
We're the fry cook burning his hand in the lunchtime rush.
We're the President rehearsing a smile in the mirror.
We're the maid scrubbing the skid marks out of his boxers.
We're the tribal elder painting patterns on our face with ash.
We're the flag, and the hand that raises it.
We're the terrorist detonating ourselves in the crowded market.

We're the cat asleep by a terracotta urn in the courtyard.
We're the disallowed goal in the final minutes.
We're the Super Bowl trophy lifted through smoke and confetti.
We're the Pope praying for a baby.
We're the cancer in the baby's blood.
We're the mustard gas drifting across an Iraqi schoolyard.
We're the beef in the stew.
We're the orangutan swinging through a shrinking canopy.
We're the CEO signing the contract to cut it all down.
We're the candle burning in the citywide blackout.
We're the kid skateboarding under a highway.
We're the bad karaoke singer in a dive bar.
We're the single mom who's going to have a one-night stand.

We're the kiss that landed wrong, and made us laugh.
We're the young lovers whose entire world is one another.

We're the mother whispering while looking at her daughter's empty
bed after curfew.
We're the ketamine the daughter is taking at the neon party.
We're the landlord counting rent in the half-light.
We're the protest banner with a slogan we stole from Reddit.
We're the silence after ambulance sirens fade.
We're the fire escape.
We're the padlock on the fire escape.
We're the last ferry leaving at midnight.
We're the graffiti that won't wash off the underpass.
We're the underpaid nurse holding the hand of the dying old man.
We're the dying old man, of course.

We're the automatic rifle in the elementary school.
We're the scarecrow in the field.
We're the field of wildflowers.
We're the border guard stamping passports in silence.
We're the silence before a verdict is read.
We're the Molotov cocktail being thrown down the street.
We're the street vendors selling roasted corn.
We're the locker that no one ever empties.
We're the table set for someone who never arrives.

We're the black box on the plane as it hurtles into the sea.
We're the jail key jingling on the prison warden's belt.

We're the lottery ticket worth two hundred million dollars.

We're the washing machine that washes the ticket.

We're the garbage truck rattling the bins.

We're the coyote I saw in the driveway last night.

We're the day breaking in pink light.

We're the sleepless dog again — barking at everything, always,

barking at nothing.

The Spirit Box - October 2015

There were ten-foot sheets leaning against the loft walls or spread across the wooden floor, the boards already lacquered with old color. He'd taped a paintbrush to the end of a pole so he could work from a distance, dragging lines and circles, faces and squares, as if afraid to get too close to the surface.

The funeral had been exactly a year ago. The car crash had been exactly thirteen months ago. His wife and daughter were buried together in her family's plot upstate.

Since then, Sirius hadn't left the city.

Friends had called a lot around the time of the funeral and in the weeks after. They dropped by, brought food, offered hugs and words of comfort. Sirius stopped answering the phone and the door, and eventually the phone stopped ringing and people stopped dropping by. The last call was maybe four months ago. Five months before that.

Grief was a weird beast. It had ravaged his life but at the same time given him just enough life to get on with. Just when Sirius felt he was getting on—opening the blinds to the sun cutting between skyscrapers outside—the beast came back and swiped at him, reminding him not to venture too far away.

Grief was a violent partner. He slept with it. Ate with it. Sat alongside it when he watched TV game shows at night. Then got beaten to a pulp by it for no discernible reason.

A year of solitary confinement had turned Sirius into a feral animal. He was unshaved. His hair was unruly and long, cut at odd angles where he trimmed it himself. He used one bowl and one fork and kept them beside the sink at all times. His duvet was on the sofa that week; his bed an unfriendly space to retreat to in the early hours.

The knock at the door came loud and unexpected.

Sirius was standing before a sheet, painting a background—black, white, gray. He blinked at the door.

He guessed whoever it was had walked away and went back to the sheet.

A louder knock now.

Sirius set down his paintbrush pole and stepped quietly toward the door. Through the peephole he saw a short man he hadn't seen for thirteen months—his agent.

Sirius stood like a statue and waited for him to walk away.

"Si, I know you're behind the door. Can you please open it?" his agent said.

Sirius didn't move.

"Si. Please. If you don't answer me it'll be the NYPD next, checking you're still alive in there."

Sirius unhooked the latch and opened the door a crack.

"Jesus," the agent said.

"Hi, Max."

"You gonna invite me in?"

Sirius considered it, then stood back and opened the door.

Max walked in. He looked like he'd just come off the golf course and had thrown a black blazer over his polo. His hair was receding to a perfect round strip around the back of his head.

"You thought about cracking a window open in here, Si?"

"What can I do for you, Max?"

"I'm not here to rescue you, if that's what you're thinking. You're a grown man, and after the tragedy you've had, you need to deal with it however you need to. If that means not answering the phone or the door for the last year, that's up to you. Having said that—if you want help, I'm here."

Sirius nodded, half in surprise, half in approval.

"So, my actual reason for being here," Max said, hitching up his trousers, "Jean called me. She's been trying to reach you for months. You're hemorrhaging money, Si. You haven't given us any new artwork. The commissions are coming in from all over, but we can't get in touch with you to get to work on them."

"So you're here for some art?"

"I'm here so you don't get your electricity shut off—which I understand is imminent."

Max wandered around the open loft, hands on his hips, leather shoes stepping over paint, brushes, rags. He looked at the giant painted sheets clipped up around the room.

"You have a series here," Max said.

A giant distorted face mid-scream hung above him.

"How many you got?" Max asked.

"Thirty, maybe forty."

"Let's put 'em to market. What do you say?"

"I have some sculptures in my storage unit too," Sirius said quietly. "Some abstract stuff—one of a chrome fish I did a few years back. They could go."

Max clapped his hands together.
"Sold!" he shouted, then dropped his smile when he saw Sirius's face.

"Seriously though, you need to get out of this apartment, Si. Everyone loves you. Everyone misses you."

Sirius nodded.

"You think…" He cleared his throat. "Ahhh, would I be able to get an advance?"

Max nodded and studied him.
"You need help—let me help. We don't need to call it an advance. How much do you need to tide you over?"

Sirius stood among the sheets of black, whites, grays, ghosts of terror surrounding them both. He scratched his face and ran a hand through his hair before he spoke.
"Enough for a plane ticket."

Then there was Bangkok in wet heat, diesel air, gold shrines wedged between phone stores. One store had a painted green apple above the door, called itself *Apple Store,* and sold flip phones.

Sirius had been sitting in two airports and two planes for over a day. He hadn't slept but had passed out from exhaustion for a few seconds on the second flight before snapping awake and apologizing to the woman beside him.

When he stepped out of the airport, everywhere was busy. Everyone moved as though they had places to be, business to take care of. Cars came from every direction.

Sirius kept moving on adrenaline: a bus to the ferry, and then a ferry to the island. He stood on the boat, deafening engines roaring, thick smoke blowing from the back. The water was turquoise and the horizon wide and clear apart from the occasional tiny island.

After three hours, the ferry pulled up to a wooden landing. Jungle climbed above the town and rolled back, high over the ocean. Everyone surged from the boat; crowds surged toward it bringing boxes and luggage before anyone else had gotten off.

Sirius had one bag — an overnight piece of luggage he'd bought in Paris with his wife before his daughter was born. Inside were rolled-up T-shirts, shorts, underwear, a small sketchbook, pencils, a photo of his family from another life — and a letter. A letter addressed to whoever might find his body, apologizing, giving Max's phone number, requesting burial with his wife and daughter.

He'd last been in Thailand thirty years earlier, when he was twenty. He was free, single, backpacking. It wasn't the place itself but the feeling of adventure that had gotten into his bones and forever changed him. It was a time he felt spiritually alive, like the universe was on his side and he knew his place within it. It seemed only right to come full circle. He didn't want to die in the loft. In the cold. In New York City. Sirius told himself he'd been dealt a bad hand, but at the very least he could control where his life would end — and he wanted it to end here.

A chalkboard advertised huts on the beach for 120 baht. *Fan only, bucket showers, lights off at midnight when the generator dies.*

He ate papaya with salt and chili and watched the paradise of white sand and perfect water. He was the oldest one staying in the huts; his neighbors were all in their twenties and thirties.

The water was how he was going to do it. He figured it was the least violent way — to wade in, head beneath the surface, a deep breath in, and then… pain? Sure. But surely unconsciousness would soon follow. Then peace. He would have escaped the beast, the violent partner.

He met Angel the second day he was there. She was small, just over five feet. Mixed heritage. She wore a loose white shirt, one sleeve rolled up, cargo trousers, and hi-top trainers. A line-work bird tattoo sat on her collarbone, a small dream catcher beside her eye, dots and lines on one wrist.

Sirius was wandering back from the market with a bottle of water. She was bent over an old cream scooter that only started when she dropped hard onto the kickstart.

She caught him looking and smiled.
"Brought back from the brink," she said in a thick South African accent.

"It's a nice scooter. Vintage," Sirius said quietly.

"It's a piece of shit," she said, "but thanks."

Sirius nodded and kept walking by.

"You're staying in the huts, right?" she called after him.

He stopped and turned around, the sun glaring in his face.

"I am," he said, forcing a small smile at the edge of his lips.

"You traveling or running?" she asked.

"Sorry?"

"I said, everyone here is either traveling or running. Which are you?"

"Passing through."

"No fair!" she said, turning off the scooter again. She wiped oil-stained hands on her trouser legs.

"What about you?" Sirius asked.

"Running. Dropped out of university. No idea what job I want to do for the rest of my life. No idea what I want to do with the rest of my life in general. So here I am."

Sirius nodded.

"My name's Angel," she said, holding one hand up to the sunlight, squinting at him.

"Sirius."

"The brightest star. Nice. You got dinner plans?"

Sirius sat in the sand at dusk and ate fish barbecued on a disposable grill with Angel and her British friend, a guy in his twenties. They talked about art and music, and Angel searched Sirius up on her phone, scrolling through his paintings.

At midnight, the lights shut off and they went back to their huts.

The next day Sirius was sitting on the back of her scooter as Angel rode the island roads. He held the rear rack with two fingers. The palms that grew wild everywhere didn't move; the heat was dry and intense. Dogs slept in the middle of the road and didn't stir as Angel rode around them.

The nights were bonfires, more barbecues, rum in plastic cups. Angel rested her head on Sirius's shoulder as they sat in the sand. He flinched as her head settled.

"Don't worry," she said. "I'm one-hundred-percent gay, Sirius."

Every night new combinations of people appeared around the fire. The huts were a constant stream of different travelers, but Angel and Sirius were the constants. People said their names and countries when they introduced themselves. The longer they stayed, Sirius noticed, the more wooden bracelets and beaded necklaces they collected.

One night around 4 a.m., Sirius woke needing to pee. It was easier and safer to use the ocean than wander from the hut to the toilets down the beach—or into the jungle behind them. At any point in the night, people stood or squatted by the tide. Sirius stepped out of the hut and walked ten steps to the water.

He peed and looked out at the moonlit ocean, rippling gently, peacefully in the humid night. He squinted at something on the horizon — a boat, maybe. A shipping container. But then there were six of them, appearing from one. They swirled around the black seam of the horizon, shot left, shot right, grew smaller and larger. One shot directly up toward the stars like a shooting star gone wrong, then streaked back down to the water, joining the others. Then they were gone.

The next night Angel told Sirius her parents had disowned her. They didn't agree with what they called her "lifestyle choices." Angel had been in love with a girl at university, but it hadn't worked out. Heartbreak made her drop out; she fled South Africa with her passport and five hundred dollars.

Sirius said he owned a two-million-dollar loft in Greenwich Village but was cash-poor. He said he'd lost his wife and daughter in a car crash the previous year. Angel didn't say anything. She put her hand on his head and pulled it gently toward her, then pushed it away — like a sister comforting a little brother.

What Sirius didn't say was that he'd brought enough money for three days. He hadn't planned to be alive on the fourth.

When the fourth day came, there were new kids in the huts and around the nightly fire. A Brazilian boy, eighteen, sat cross-legged, fiddling with a small electronic device in his hands.

"You can talk to spirits with this thing," he said in the tone of a child opening a Christmas present.

Angel asked where he'd bought it. He said he got it from a store on the other side of the island for a hundred baht.

"It's called a spirit box," he said.

Sirius drew patterns in the sand with a stick, removing himself from the conversation. Two Australians with sunburn and a German girl with her Irish boyfriend sat nearby.

"Ask it something," the Brazilian kid said to Angel.

"Like what?" she asked.

"Anything."

She asked nothing and joked that he'd been scammed for a hundred baht.

The Brazilian asked the dead for their name.

Static rose and fell from the box. It crackled like an old radio searching for a station.

The group, illuminated only by fire and moon, watched the box. It felt stupid—and then it didn't. Smiles and rolling eyes became straight faces, eyes fixed on the sound.

"Is anybody there?" one of the Australians asked.

The fire spat.

The lights from the huts shut off, marking midnight.

Sirius wiped away the pattern he'd drawn and started a new one.

"Ask it again," the Brazilian said.

"Is anybody there?"

From the static came a stutter of a syllable, a fragment of a voice.

— OME

The Australians laughed too loudly, and the German girl folded into her boyfriend's chest, his arms around her.

"Again!" the Brazilian said.

Angel looked over at Sirius.
"Maybe we should go, Sirius," she said.

A sudden loud scrape of static burst from the radio into the night. Everyone flinched—except Sirius.

DON'T

A beat of silence. Then:

LOVE.

Sirius rose to his feet and walked fast down the beach until he was away from the glow of the fire. His cry broke from him in a breath that tore from his throat. He sat in the wet sand and let the water wash in around him. Angel came down the beach, not running but walking toward him.

She didn't ask if he was okay. She sat beside him in the tide, and the water swept in and swept out.

Sirius cried heavily, shoulders shaking. It was the first time he had cried since the crash.

"I don't know why I'm here," he said.

"You do," Angel said. "You're here to grieve. That's okay."

Sirius shook his head, wiping his eyes with his wrists.
"No. That's not what I mean. I came here to end it all. I was going to fucking drown myself in the sea. I should be dead now. I can't go on with this heartache."

Angel didn't respond. She sat beside him, looking out at the dark ocean, her shoulder touching his.

"That day of the crash," Sirius said, "we were coming back from a dinner party. My daughter had been restless all evening. My wife and I argued while I was driving home. I said something about how meeting her was pure chance. I told her she was a fucking curse to me. That I was happier before I met her. I said it in front of our daughter in the back seat. My daughter's eyes were looking at me in the rearview mirror… Jesus Christ… she was ten years old and looked at me with fear. I can't stop seeing that look. I can't fucking live with it anymore. I was still shouting while I was driving. I was angry. Then I lost control. The car clipped the side of the road. It sounded like a bomb going off. We rolled so many times and then… I came out with a couple of scratches. I knew from the silence they were dead."

The surf folded in.

"People say cruel things," Angel said softly. "Just because you said something doesn't mean it defines an entire life. They knew you loved them, I'm sure."

A scream and a laugh carried from the bonfire down the beach.

"You think that thing is real?" Sirius asked.

Angel shrugged.
"I think if you listen to static long enough, you'll hear patterns in it — in people, in the water. That's what grief is. Everything takes another shape, right? People pretend it's God, something divine coming through, when it's just… noise. It doesn't make it any less meaningful."

Sirius laughed, breathless, still crying.
"You think I should go home?" he asked.

"You should. You should take that message with you — from the box. Your story shouldn't end here in this water, Sirius."

"There's nothing waiting for me at home, though."

"Then build it. Grief is something you can't wallow in. I don't mean to be harsh, man, but it gets to a point where grieving becomes a choice."

"How do you know all this stuff?" Sirius asked, half-laughing, wiping tears away.

"The girl at university I told you about? It wasn't that it didn't work out. She hanged herself."

Sirius looked over at her, then back at the water.

"That message from the box — I thought it was for me," Angel said, laughing once, then breaking into a cry.

Sirius placed his arm around her shoulder, and they sat there.

The lights out at sea appeared and shifted. He imagined a beast's hands reaching through all that dark water and all that mistaken distance — not finding him because he'd moved to a new place where they could no longer reach him.

Angel stood and offered her hand. He took it.

They walked back up the beach. The Australians and the Brazilian were arguing about something that would never matter.

The German girl was French kissing her boyfriend.

The spirit box was still crackling in the sand.

The Better Place - May 2016

So,
maybe
we should
take a moment
and
breathe.

Take
a break
from wearing
our hearts
on our sleeve,
and
take
the
fight
down
to
the
people.

There's
a kid
getting
thrown
out of the
club
tonight.

He's
swinging wild
at the
bouncer
with
all
of
his might.

He's
screaming
about
losing his phone.
He's
screaming
about
his
friends
leaving.

And
all
along
there's
the
constant
after-
shock —
hearts
beating

along
to
the
cosmic
clock.

The
constant
expanding
universe.
The
lights
flash,
and
the
crowds
disperse.

I'm
going
to
a
better place.
Happiness
I'll
never
again
misplace.

Neon
paint
glowing
bright
across
our
faces.

Now
the
sky's
tearing
open
across
the
horizon.
The
tide's
breaking
cold
around
our ankles.

We're
high
on
molly,
Haribo,
and
beer.

I
raise
my hands
and
shout,

**"WHAT
HORROR
IT
WAS
TO
FIND
OUT
WE
HAD
FREE
WILL!"**

But
I'm
coming
around
to the idea —
if
I
have
it,
I
guess
I'll

use
it.

But still,
I'm
going
to
that
better
place.
We're
getting
out of
the
damn
rat
race,
sailing
away
toward
something
kinder.

Now
watch
the
group chat
lose
its
mind —

un-
read
posts
left
be-
hind.

I
hope
this
doesn't
hurt
now.
I'm
going
to a
better
place,
re-
playing
the
same old
video
games.

It's
Right,
X,
Right,
Left,

Right,

R1,

Right,

Left,

X,

Triangle.

I

don't

think

this

will

be

my

master-

piece —

a

dying art,

a

limited release.

At

twenty-

eight,

I'm

really

over

the

hill

now,

sell-

ing

my

heart-

break

like

a

pros-

ti-

tute,

for

someone

to

read

on

the

morn-

ing

com-

mute.

The

winter

sun's

hitting

the

window

sill.

And still,
I'm
going
to
a
better
place —
an
empty
chair,
a
shivering
face.

But
it's
all
okay,
it's
all
really
chill.

I'm
performing
that
final scene,
taking
a bow
as

the
up-
and-
coming-
once-
great-
has-
been.

The
curtain
drops.
The applause
never
comes.

But
just
in
case
this
is
our
last
embrace —
do
me
a
favor:

Tear

these

pages

out.

Now eat them.

The Debate - March 2018

"Ladies and Gentlemen, all the way from Rhode Island, we have the host of the podcast *This Isn't A Safe Space*, banned from numerous college campuses during his lecture tour last year. Some call him alt-right, some call him far right, some just call him simply, a troll. Please welcome to the stage Mr. Scoot Brewer."

He came out on the tiny stage wearing dark blue jeans, a blue blazer, shirt, tie, and a MAGA hat. Some of the students booed him, but most clapped.

He smiled and waved at the crowd, pointed at those he saw booing, and drew a sad face on his mouth with his finger. A couple of guys whooped. A girl in the front row turned her back to him in protest, pulled a blindfold over her eyes, and folded her arms.

The next person introduced was a student representative, head of the political debate society — Skye, a girl with curly red hair wearing army boots with a summer dress. She got a similar amount of boos and cheers, which I didn't expect. I figured for the right-wing American guy walking into a British university student debate, even as a special guest, would be like a snake entering a cage full of mongooses. But apparently, Skye — young, female, leftist, and outspoken — carried her own baggage with this crowd.

They took their seats: two tub chairs on either side of a small table with one jug of water and two glasses.

Scoot immediately reached into his inside pocket and palmed something that couldn't be seen. He held it to his lips and blew out a plume of smoke.

The adjudicator, a woman from the University holding a tablet and sitting on a chair to the side of the stage, caught it from the corner of her eye.

"Mr. Brewer, we must ask that you don't vape while inside the building, thank you," she said. A scattering of boos came from the crowd again.

Scoot smiled without showing any teeth and placed the vape back into his inside pocket.

"Cherry. Cherry flavor if anyone was wondering," he said into his mic.

Someone shouted something from the crowd.

"What's that?" Scoot said, narrowing his eyes through the spotlight. "Blueberry? Yeah, I fuck with Blueberry too. I'm sort of busy right now, man, so how about we talk vape juice later, okay?"

There was a ripple of laughter and a couple more boos. One guy shouted "loser" to the stage.

The adjudicator cleared her throat and gave some background on Skye — she was a twenty-one-year-old politics and history major at the University and had represented the student body in parliamentary groups with MPs. Scoot was a twenty-eight-year-old college dropout with a large social media presence. His most popular video was him at a college debate in the U.S. where he carefully dismantled a student's pro-stance on diversity and equality. I'd seen the video a while ago and had been struck by his charisma and humor. If I was a young white male, seeing another young white male with such confidence, bravado, and — what looked like — intelligence, I could easily have been sold into thinking he was speaking for me when nobody else in the world seemed to be. He vaped throughout that video too.

"Can I just say," Scoot said, interrupting the adjudicator, "thank you so much, Skye, for dressing up for tonight's debate. Those boots make it look like you're auditioning for 'angry extra number twelve' in *Les Misérables*."

There was laughter again, a ripple moving through the room.

Skye smiled. She was sitting slightly forward on her chair while Scoot sat upright like he was sitting on a throne.

"Between the two of us," Skye said into her microphone, "if you want to get into dress sense, I don't think you'd want to pull that thread, looking at what you're wearing. Your hat was made in China, by the way."

Cheers erupted in the lecture hall. A couple of students stamped their boots on the floor.

"Yeah, it's made in China," Scoot said into his mic while grinning, disrupting the roll of applause. "It's not, but let's not let facts get in the way of a good sound bite, right Sly — sorry, Skye? It is Skye, right?"

Skye blinked away from him, rolled her eyes, and looked at the adjudicator.

The debate started off with the question: *How can diversity and equality initiatives be advanced in a way that includes everyone?*

Skye spoke eloquently about there being a myth that D&E policies were anti-white or anti-male, and that those with misogynistic or racist agendas used this as a means to whip up anger. She argued it was just about bringing those who have historically been left behind up to an equal starting point for opportunities.

She spoke calmly, slowly, in sentences that sounded like they'd been written first and memorized — the kind of phrasing you imagine highlighted in a student society group chat. She even folded her hands in her lap when she'd finished speaking, like she was presenting a thesis to a panel.

Scoot didn't wait a beat. He leaned forward into his mic like a boxer leaning into a punch.

"Okay, but here's the thing," he said, and already I could feel the crowd tense — they knew he had his act lined up. Those who loved him were waiting for it just as eagerly as those who hated him. "If diversity and equality are so important, why don't you let a disabled Black woman sit in your seat tonight? Why do you get to talk for her? You're white, you're privileged, you're sitting on stage, and you're telling me you're the voice of equality. That's not equality. I'm here because I'M THE BEST QUALIFIED PERSON TO BE HERE."

The boos and claps came at the same time, like a weather front.

He wasn't done. "And let me remind you all — working-class white boys do the worst in schools in your country. Not Black kids. Not Asian kids. White boys. Nobody talks about them, do they? Where's the parade? Where's the awareness month? Where's the hashtag for them?"

Half the crowd clapped, the other half shouted insults, and I sat there wondering how I'd become an audience member in a pantomime.

Skye leaned forward now, her hand slicing the air. "You can throw statistics around, but the reality is white men — of all classes and ages — still hold the majority of power in politics, in business, in media, in culture. You think equality means losing something. It doesn't. It means sharing it."

Applause. A couple of students actually stood up to clap, like they'd been waiting for their fighter to get off the ropes and swing back.

Scoot grinned and held his hands up in mock surrender. "Sharing it. Okay. So when is it my turn to get years of maternity leave but expect the same pay rise?"

That got a ripple of laughter and boos again. That was his trick, I'd realized — please half of them, enrage half of them, throw in some humor, throw in one fact for every five opinions, and when any of them stumbles, pounce with something brutal to win every time (the brutal thing didn't even have to be true).

The adjudicator tried to move things on, clearing her throat in an attempt to summon authority. "Thank you, both. Perhaps we can turn to immigration."

This was Scoot's playground. He licked his lips like a man about to tuck into veal.

Skye, to her credit, went first. She spoke about compassion, about treating every immigrant as vulnerable, about hospitality and dignity as a human right. You could hear her sincerity even under the growing nerves.

Scoot waited, hands folded like a priest. When she finished, he asked, "What, even the rapey ones?"

Gasps, boos, cheers — the full cycle again. He spread his arms like Jesus on the cross and basked in the noise.

He doubled down. "Don't act shocked. Don't. You all know what I'm saying. We open the doors, we let everyone in, and then we're supposed to just say thank you? No questions asked? You want Sweden 2.0? No? Didn't think so."

The crowd erupted — half yelling, half clapping. I could feel my own pulse in my ears.

Skye's voice cracked with anger. "You're not talking about non-humans when you talk about immigrants. You're talking about people. Families. Children. And you stand up here reducing them to one word because it suits your agenda. That's not debate. That's hate."

Thunderous cheers. Stamping feet.

Scoot leaned back like a man sunbathing. "Oh! There it is. The magic word. Hate. It was almost the 'r' word — racism — but you stopped just short. The golden ticket. The ace card. If you can't beat me with arguments, you brand me with hate. You think that shuts me down? It doesn't. It proves I'm right and you're losing."

He sipped water, deliberately, like he'd just served a knockout blow. About four guys in the back actually started a chant of "SCOOT, SCOOT, SCOOT" that quickly stopped.

At this point, the debate wasn't about policy anymore. It was about volume. Whenever Skye spoke, half the room mumbled and jeered while the other half shouted them down. Whenever Scoot spoke, the roles swapped. The whole hall had become a theater of petty noise.

And then Scoot delivered a line that I didn't think I'd ever hear: "I'll tell you the real crisis in immigration. The shortage of big booty Latinas in the UK."

The line, most likely rehearsed, detonated the room. It somehow got both the loudest boo and the loudest cheer.

I rubbed my temples. I had a headache. I'd thought this would be an interesting debate — good versus evil. But I quickly realized, to my dismay, there was no right or wrong shining through. There was just noise and anger and sound bites. It was a circus — only we, the audience, were the clowns.

And then, faintly, like a whisper, came the smell.

At first, it was nothing — like a candle wick left smoking after the flame died. I might not have noticed it if the girl next to me hadn't leaned over and whispered, "Do you smell that?"

I nodded and gave her a *yeah, I do, but there's no alarm going off so I guess we're in an unquantifiable amount of danger at the moment* expression that I hoped she read.

But the smell didn't go away. It thickened. It lodged in throats. People coughed and laughed at the same time.

Skye stopped mid-sentence. "Everyone else smells that too, right?" she said with a laugh that wobbled at the edges.

"Smell what?" Scoot asked, poker-faced.

"Erm, the smoke. You can't smell it?"

"Oh. Yeah, there's no smell of smoke," Scoot said confidently and crossed his legs. He reached into his inside pocket, took a puff of his vape, and exhaled a cherry cloud across the table.

"MR. BREWER, again I must ask you not to vape on the premises!" the adjudicator barked.

But this wasn't vape smoke. This was thicker, darker, curling into the spotlights. A cough broke out in the front row. Another in the middle. Then laughter. Nervous. Half-crazed. The crowd was moving closer to the line of hysteria, and the line was blurring by the second.

The crowd started to shift, rising, craning necks toward the exits. Some students strapped on backpacks like soldiers about to flee. Others stayed put, eyes wide, too committed to the spectacle to abandon it.

Scoot spotted them and pounced.

"Look at them. We're gonna have to think of a slur for the ones who can smell the smoke. The Smoke Sniffers. First sign of danger, they're gone. They don't like the smell, so they run. That's your future, folks." He leaned back, legs crossed, and blew another cherry halo. "Me? I stay."

The hall cracked in two again — laughter, boos, cheers, coughing. A girl clutched her inhaler while the boy next to her slammed his hands together in applause for Scoot.

The smoke was no longer a rumor. It was a presence. It crawled down the aisles, clung to hair, seeped into denim jackets. Students got their phones out and started livestreaming it.

Skye stood up, a hand on her hip, and looked at the smoke curling into the room.

"You know what this is," Scoot said. "When you've lost the argument, you start shouting 'fire!' It's a classic neo-liberal strategy."

"How can it be both classic and neo-liberal, you fucking moron?" Skye said before throwing the microphone back into her empty chair.

The adjudicator stood up and moved to the edge of the stage. "Ladies and Gentlemen, we're going to pause the debate here because I understand some of us are concerned about the smoke. Please remain calm and seated, and I'm going to go and see if we need to leave the building. Thank you."

Scoot shook his head and reached back into his inside pocket for his vape.

Skye sat on the arm of her chair, shaking her head at the crowd that was now talking loud, some standing, some moving to the aisles.

The adjudicator walked down the steps from the stage and out of the double doors.

"Can I just say," Scoot said — even his voice on the mic was being lost among the noise of the crowd — "Can I just say! Look at that! Look up there! What are those, huh? What are those!?"

He pointed up to the ceiling and the crowd only grew louder when they saw he was pointing at sprinklers. Some of the crowd laughed and applauded; others shouted with anger back at him.

Skye picked up her microphone and spoke. "Hey guys, someone should just set off the fire alarm. We should all leave. This isn't safe."

Scoot laughed hysterically off the mic before holding it to his lips again. "You do it! You push the alarm if you're so concerned! Why are you still here anyway?"

Half the crowd cheered.

"I want to make sure everyone is safe first," Skye said, and the other half of the crowd cheered in response.

"Where's the woman who hates my vape? The fuck did she go?" Scoot said, looking around toward the double doors. "Where'd that chick go? She's been like ten minutes, right?"

Half the crowd laughed, spluttering.

Now the stage belonged to Scoot and Skye. She perched on the arm of her chair, knuckles white around the mic. He sat cross-legged, calm as a monk, smirking in the growing haze of smoke.

The smoke grew denser, swallowing the first few rows, blurring the exits. Phone torches went on like fireflies.

Skye shouted something about safety — she said someone should raise the alarm, someone should make the leap and evacuate first — her voice cracking in the thick air. Scoot countered with something about immigration and waterboarding, and half the room clapped.

The rage grew in the room. People were shouting at each other and pushing each other back and forth. I managed to get out of the row and against a wall but still took an elbow to the face from one of the hundreds shifting side to side, shouting at one another in the growing dark.

Then the sprinklers came to life and the loudest alarm I'd ever heard started blaring.

Gallons of water sprayed down on the crowd that were just openly fighting one another now. Their shouts and screams drowned out by the alarm.

I pushed through the crowd, got pushed back, and pushed forward again until I got to the door where people started breaking through.

The cold water had soaked everything and everyone.

I stepped through the doors to the lobby of the auditorium. The lobby had giant thirty-foot-high glass walls, and it was clear there was smoke billowing past outside. The student union next door was on fire.

Wailing of fire engines could be heard now, and hundreds from other lecture halls were filing past under the scream of the alarms.

The adjudicator hadn't returned. It didn't seem like she was ever returning. She had bailed on the wreckage of her own authority, vanished into the haze like a bureaucratic ghost, leaving us to argue inside a burning room.

Onstage, Skye stayed sitting on the arm of her chair, telling people they should leave. Scoot blew cherry-scented halos into the thickening dark, and somewhere in the smoke, the unnatural darkness, the rain of the sprinklers, the coughing and the chaos, I swear he made eye contact with me and mouthed the words:

Smoke Sniffer.

The Anarchy Ending - September 2018

Ellie told me on the plane that the hotel was going to be the fanciest hotel she had ever stayed at.

"It's a good one," I said. "You'll enjoy it."

We'd only been together for a month or so. We didn't share much except for drinking and taking whatever drugs came our way in bathrooms, bars, friends' houses, and rooftops. Being in self-destruct mode, it turns out, was enough to bond us. The attraction was never sexual, not at first. It was more like when you meet someone at school and think *You. You're going to be my friend. We can get into trouble together.*

The hotel looked like a palace sitting next to the Mediterranean, all white stone beneath the hot sun. There were terraces with palms everywhere; the staff all wore dark green waistcoats and bow ties. A private beach sat beyond the pool, just a rough track leading through the sand from the terrace.

Inside, everything was just as palatial: chandeliers, marble, five elegant restaurants, wide corridors with lines of gold running down them like veins. A koi pond was beside the reception where the fish did their steady, unbothered circles as if they were on the payroll.

We checked in, fried from the flight, and left the bags just inside the door. We immediately hit the bar.

The haze pulled in gently, from the edges, like it generally did.

The first drink sank the shoulders. The second eased the mind. By
the third, the fourth, you lose count. Then there were snapshots of
images: her laughing with strangers, putting an arm around me,
kissing me, pushing my face away. She called me dramatic at one
point and overly sensitive, and I got angry and upset. Then we were
laughing again. There were new strangers buying us drinks.

I woke up in the next moment, not sure what day it was or what time
it was. It was dark. I was fully clothed and curled up on the very
edge of the bed. Ellie lay on her back, stretched out beside me,
unconscious, her blonde hair across her face.

I stretched, walked over to the balcony doors, and opened them. The
ocean was black and quiet, the sound of its pull and push the only
sound in the world.

The moon set a thin white line on the horizon, and above it, I saw
what I first thought was a plane, the flickering yellow lights. They
moved fast, sideways across the horizon — miles a second, probably
— then quickly shot vertical to the heavens before vanishing. I
stayed watching the night, breathing the cool air into my lungs.

I closed the balcony doors, pulled the curtains closed, and crawled
back onto the bed.

The next day we woke just before lunch. We ate, hit the beach,
played in the ocean, shouting and screaming and laughing with one
another. At night, we were back in the bar. The first drink, the second

drink, the third, the fourth… then there was the koi pond.

We were in it somehow, soaking wet, wearing our evening dress-code clothes. I was worried about hurting the fish and shouted at her to stop when she kept kicking water to splash me.

In my addled mind, I took it personally. When the staff shouted at us to get out and stop disturbing the koi, I took their side and told them they should throw her out. What I failed to realize, in that moment, was that the staff hated me equally and were likely considering throwing us both out.

"Why are you so stressed?" she said, and grabbed hold of my dripping-wet shoulders.

She pouted, cupped my face, and kissed my lips.

I forgave her immediately and was firmly back on her side, the koi be damned.

We were escorted, dripping wet, back to our room and told firmly by the manager that we were not to leave for the rest of the night. A security guard was stationed outside the door, on a chair, all night.

"You think it would be fucked up if I ordered room service?" she asked.

"I think it would be fucked up, yes. You nearly killed their koi, Ellie."

"Me? I nearly killed their koi? I didn't nearly kill their koi. You pushed me in first."

I thought back. Maybe I had. There was no way of knowing. I was

 too drunk to know whether I was being gaslighted or not, too tired
to care.

We lay on top of the bed in our underwear, our heads touching
gently, and talked into the night.

She told me all the best artists die young and unknown.

I thanked her for that, said it was heartening to hear.

"Do you ever feel like it's all coming to a natural end?" she asked. It
was the most honest she'd been with me.

"I've felt that way before. When I've lost people I loved. But you
eventually realize that everything is fragile and so it works both
ways. You may easily lose your reason to stay alive but then, out of
nowhere, when you least expect it, there's a new reason that appears
from the ether."

"What's your reason right now?" she asked.

Without thinking, I said,

"That I've got a whole other chapter of my life waiting after this
horrible one closes."

I didn't consider until after the response of silence that she may have
hoped I'd give her as my reason.

The next evening, we learned the hotel reserves the right, per the small print, to cut certain guests off that were "exhibiting unsafe behavior."

The manager read it to us in the same tone a priest might speak to a prisoner before the executioner's fire. We took our unsafe behavior elsewhere that night.

We got a taxi into the local town and found alcohol and drugs there. The familiar haze settled in again and the night became another carousel of images — staggering into the street, a car stopping just short of hitting me, an angry driver yelling at me in a foreign language as I apologized, heads down over a closed toilet seat in a cubicle, spinning in circles under strobe lights, bass music, a man spilled a drink that partly landed on me and he laughed, I pushed him, large arms of a bouncer around my shoulder, Ellie screaming at someone, a bottle being thrown, a window smashing, running, tripping, grazing my hands.

We went into another club and then there was Ellie laughing, hugging me, kissing me, her mouth tasting of cigarettes and something metallic. She said something about going back to the hotel, she said something about what she wanted to do to me.

As the sky shifted from purple to a pale blue, we stumbled into the hotel room, kissing, pulling at each other's clothes, collapsing onto the bed.

The curtains were half open. Outside, the sea kept moving, calm and steady.

She was on top of me, rocking to an unheard rhythm, her back arching as the first line of golden sunlight cut through the gap in the curtains and caught one of my eyes.

By the next night, we were still coming down, the two of us a tangled wreckage that was now haunting the hotel, floating through it with no sense of direction, no idea how to fill our days now that the bar was closed to us.

By the final night, we had been sober for days.

We sat quietly on a wall outside the hotel, sitting in the shade of a palm tree, waiting for the car to pick us up to take us back to the airport.

"This was fun," she said.

"It was," I said.

"Why do I get the sense that we're not talking about the vacation?"

"We're probably not healthy for one another right now," I said. "I mean it, you know. It was fun. It's just, things don't last forever."

She squeezed my hand and smiled at me, and I smiled back.

"That's where you're wrong" she said "some things do last forever. You just haven't found that thing yet."

On the plane, she slept with her mouth open, slouched up against the window. The attendant offered me a drink and I said no.

Clouds were slowly moving beneath us as we flew.

Last night, the final night, I'd kind of baptized myself in the hotel bathtub. I'd dunked my head beneath the water and broke back above the surface. Dunked my head again and broke back up again. I'd made a pact that things couldn't go on like this; there had to be something else, something better, something worthwhile.

If this was a perfect story and I was a perfect narrator, this would be the part where I told you I got my shit together. I took my free will and set out to create, achieve, do better, and return back home to California with a renewed philosophy, a whole new way of being.

But things don't happen overnight. Sometimes they can take years.

I'd taken the first step.

I just needed to take another one tomorrow.

Then one after that.

I gave myself permission to stumble or fall completely but only on the understanding I had to get back onto the path.

To stay focused and to live toward a better life.

If this was a perfect story and I was a perfect narrator, this is the part where the plane would crash.

How I Spent My Covid Vacation - July 2019

I was forty minutes from midnight when I took the first sip of absinthe.

I'd been given half a bottle earlier in the evening by a man I'd only met that afternoon.

"Never tried it," he said. "You mean never?"

It was true — I'd never tried absinthe but had read a lot about its mythology. Victorian madmen were crazy for the stuff. They spoke of hallucinations, sentient shadows, and yes, green fairies. This was all worth the price of admission alone.

The man with absinthe lived in a scurrilous, ramshackle house about a forty-minute drive to Woodland Hills. I'd made the journey as I was all out of weed, and one of the kids where I worked had pointed me in absinthe man's direction a couple of weeks ago.

Finally, I took his advice and made the drive. It was a Monday, after all. I was writing again. The sun was still shining, although there were strong winds that made it feel more like late summer than July.

As well as this, the whole world had been in lockdown for the last four months due to the coronavirus plague.

I'd survived it by doing little other than going to the beach, drinking beer daily at home, and doing odd bits of work for a downtown L.A. youth programme. The job, it turned out, was the perfect job to have in the middle of a pandemic. My main task was: let the kids get on with it and don't cough on anyone.

I mastered this.

The kids smoked dope while I did my drugs outside of the mission, then spent my shifts reading and having the odd conversation with a teenager, encouraging them everything will be okay. They had to choose good, the ying and yang and all that stuff,..

The job also meant I continued getting 100% of my salary plus benefits for working through a pandemic. This put me in a better position than much of the country. The majority were not working, and the minority who were, were in the deep of it — the nurses, food workers, teachers. The ones whose jobs meant that in the theater of society, their seats were firmly behind a pillar up in the rafters at the back.

My job meant I wasn't up there, but I also wasn't by any means on the front row or in the royal boxes — that was, as always, reserved for the rich and the government. No, I was where I liked to be. To the side, on the edges, looking in.

After four months of sitting there on the edges, the pandemic was easing. The public were being urged to go outside. I'd made enough money to buy a laptop to start writing again. It was all going to plan.

So to blow off the cobwebs and make the new start — that I wanted to feel like the old start — I felt the best place to start was weed.

It'd free me up. Settle me down. Give me time and space to think and stop worrying about distractions.

In the end, I haggled for $50 worth of weed from absinthe man and, in his shock that I had never tried absinthe, he gifted me a little under half a bottle.

"Thanks, man," I muttered and held the bottle up to the crack of light shining into the house.

"It ain't green like on TV," he said.

I had never seen absinthe on TV and highly doubted he had.

"Best absinthe has more of a pale color. Too green and it means it has coloring added to it. No good."

I nodded and raised my eyebrows. He had genuinely taught me something.

We'd got to the point in our contact where there was nowhere else to go. I'd got what I wanted. He'd got what he wanted. I suddenly became very aware he was wearing no shirt, he was overweight, and his areolas were huge.

"Well," I said, "I ought to go."

Within seconds, I was back in my car, pushed it into gear, and roared off, back south, down the Pacific Coast Highway, just the ocean to the right of me and the unseasonal July wind blowing through my hair. "Helter Skelter" blasted on the radio. I'd buckled the seatbelt in over the pale green absinthe sitting in the seat beside me for no reason. No reason at all.

Now I'd taken my first sip and hated the stuff. It was bitter and chemical-like. I took another sip.

I was vaguely aware I had to be awake at 7 a.m. the next morning as my job was going back to normal. No more late nights. No more early finishes. No more getting in late. No more doing nothing.

As well as not being ready for this, I also had no intention — none — of doing this. The job was well-paid, sure. It had got me through the winter and a global plague, sure. But Goddamn it, I wasn't climbing into bed on a balmy Monday night in July, setting my alarm clock, while I had half a bottle of absinthe, $50 of weed, and ecstasy I'd bummed from work.

I'd also got Xanax from work, but Xanax gave a high I didn't want or need, and I'd flushed them when I'd found them among the baggie of colorful Es I'd obtained.

I'd started writing too — a punk novel. I wasn't interested in money, I was only interested in legacy at this point.

If I took care of having fun, being easy, lucky, free, my legacy would take care of itself. So everything I did, each decision I made, was based on what I'd always used to base it on — *is this going to be a cool story to tell?* If the answer wasn't yes, I wasn't interested. Hence the job in the youth programme. Hence restarting writing. Hence no longer caring about money. I was taking steps to something higher.

By midnight, the absinthe had hit me. I was a flat-out drunk, literally, lying on the floor listening to the *Nitro Circus* documentary play on a TV that was a few feet away but sounded like it was in a room two houses away. My senses and perception of everything around me were off-kilter. The room wasn't spinning, but it was tilting — a gentle tilt right, and then a gentle tilt left. My body moved involuntarily with the motion of my swaying room.

It would have been easy to lie there and ignore the creeping wave of euphoria I felt coming and go to sleep, waking up ten hours later, three hours late for work.

No, I needed to ride this. I needed to bond my job, the money, with my mantra.

Is this going to be a cool story to tell?

Going to sleep on the floor and getting fired was not a cool story.

I rolled over to my knees and managed to stagger to my feet. The euphoria started to roll back again as the unbalanced, fried senses took over.

"I need music," I said to myself. "I need shoes."

I hadn't taken a euphoric high in some time and this, I could feel, was going to be quite something. I had to make the most of it. Ride it. Soak it in. Wake myself up. That had been the whole point of buying the weed in the first place. Lacing it in THC was just a byproduct of the point. The absinthe was an unexpected attendee. The MDMA I was about to swallow was just me announcing myself as being back — living free, living fun, but living smart.

I grabbed my iPad after pulling on my Nikes and headed for the front door. The instant hit of balmy night air — but still that Pacific July breeze — immediately started the euphoria crashing back. I had to get to the beach before it hit. This was the only good way to do this.

The streets were dark and quiet. Even places that used to be open all night no longer served past 7 p.m. The plague was still out there.

The beach was fifty paces from my house. It too was dark and quiet.

Only the waves crashing onto the beach could be heard, the low hum of a generator for one of the closed seafront businesses.

The top of the beach was lit by the promenade lights. The dark palm trees swayed in the wind. The far end of the beach, where the waves were crashing on the shore, was in darkness. Beyond that, the black of the sea. A couple of boats in the distance with single lights on. Beyond that, the city curling around the coast — its skyscrapers lit up red, blue, with countless window lights and street lamps no bigger than a single pencil point in the distance.

I moved down the stairs to the beach. The wind and fresh air had woken my senses a bit more and the world was no longer tilting.

Instead, I felt a calmness. A still, profound calmness that made me feel I was not floating but absolutely comfortable with being on my two feet. Each step I took on the sand felt good. Little sparks of electricity shot up my legs with each step I took, and my breathing became calm. Sure. I had no tension, I had no ill will. I was there.

My mind was open and ready. The wave had hit.

I continued walking into the gradual darkness of the beach, toward the shoreline, and without consciously thinking about it, placed my iPad in the sand and kept walking into the sea. It was cold, but it was what it was.

I lay backward and floated on the waves, only a foot or so from the shore. I drifted out farther and baptized myself — putting my head under the dark water once. Then twice. I felt awoken.

It was floating there in the darkness of the water, looking out at the city, that I realized I hadn't changed at all. Nothing had come along to shake me off my path as I had defeated all the things that had previously tried.

I didn't need to keep climbing higher as I was already high. High enough to write. High enough to drive to some hillbilly with giant nipples forty minutes away and buy drugs and get absinthe from him. High enough to be here in this water right now thinking about all of this.

All I needed to be now was to be. To keep myself on this path. To impart it. To be the personification of it — of easiness, of luckiness, of freedom.

I smiled and then laughed. I continued laughing and lay back in the water looking up to the stars. I guess what I'm trying to say is I'm doing alright.

I had to keep this peacefulness. I couldn't lose it. This was what I had come here for, and I had found it.

I lay there and rested. The darkness. The waves. The coldness. The warmth. The lights.

I got to my feet and walked back to the beach.

I sat on the sand, opened my iPad, and took out the lone joint I had in there. I lit it and played Leonard Cohen — *There Is a Crack in Everything.*

Just me. And you. And everything else.

Halo Part One - January 2021

When I met Halo, he was the undercard — hustling as a support act for some TikTok rapper who made the bulk of his money streaming himself playing video games. Two hundred and fifty bodies, without COVID masks, packed into the back of a little art gallery in Mid-Wilshire. The weed smoke hung thick in the air.

Halo came out shirtless. His belly was slick with sweat and his jowls shone under the cheap stage lights. A gold chain the size of a tow rope swung from his neck and slapped his chest. The sound system was trash — you could only make out half of his words, and the bass tore the amps into a howl of feedback. None of it mattered, though — the crowd had their hands raised and chanted along.

By the time the headliner came on, the weed fog had gotten too much and I dipped just before midnight. Outside, it was L.A. winter cold — not real cold — and I found Halo, still shirtless but now with a baseball cap on, doubled over and retching at the base of a palm tree. His T-shirt was clutched in one hand, his other hand clawed onto his knee.

There was no vomit from what I could see — he was just very stoned.

"You good?" I asked.

He put a thumb into the air without looking. A delivery robot wheeled its way past us both and had to navigate tentatively around a dry-retching Halo. His jeans kept sagging and showed more of his ass crack every time he heaved.

Eventually, he straightened up and looked at me. His eyes were watering and red. He slid the shirt on and yanked the chain back out so it was on view.

"You see the show?" he asked.

"Yeah, you were great."

"What's that accent? Australian?"

"British."

"Ahh, okay."

"You from L.A.?"

"Born and raised," he said. "Glendale."

Halo took out a plastic tube from the pocket of his jeans, opened the top, and slid out a giant joint. He put the tube back, removed a box of matches, struck one, and lit the end.

"You see that dude after me?"

"The headliner?"

"Yeah, man got famous playing *Mario Kart*. That's his art and now he thinks he's Pac. What's up with that?"

"Maybe you should stream video games too?"

"Nah. I ain't about that. My EP is out — I just need enough people to hear that, get some more bookings, and things will take off for me."

"What's the EP called?"

"Half Price Wings."

"Nice."

"Oh yeah, you like that? I got the idea at a Buffalo Wings place. They had this chicken wing promo poster on the wall — it was a wing with angel wings, a halo, and a harp. I thought, *fuck, that's meant to be, right? God's sending me signs right there.* So it was *Half Price Wings.*"

"It feels honest, at least."

Halo nodded and blew out a plume of smoke.

"You wanna get some food?" he asked. "There's an all-night diner over there."

The diner was retro-themed, full of Americana, booths with red padded seating, and a metal napkin dispenser on each table.

Halo slouched into a booth and glanced at the laminated menu, flipped it over, and handed it to me. A sleep-deprived-looking waitress sauntered over to the table holding a tablet and stylus.

Halo spoke like he was giving important instructions, holding up a different finger every time he named a new part of the order:

"Lemme get a stack of pancakes — make 'em stupid thick. Can I get 'em with cream cheese frosting, extra bacon, and can I get enough syrup so I can drown 'em? Chocolate milk to drink."

I ordered pancakes and a Coke.

"What do you want from what you're doing?" I asked.

Halo thought for a long time.

"Money. Fame. Power. I wanna get out of the condo I share with my mom, ya know? I wanna be surrounded by my own crew. House in the Hills with a pool. Maybach in the drive. All that."

"Someone once told me that the most you could want from whatever your art is, is that it just allows you to stay real — stay making art."

Halo shook his head, and without looking at me, said,

"Nah, that's bullshit. You gotta get what's coming to you. I was born in Glendale. My mom had to move constantly and we were homeless living at my aunt's house for a couple of years. Now I ain't got any college degree, I don't have any seed money, I don't have any assets. *Half Price Wings* is the only asset I truly own. Where your rich kids put their privilege to work to accumulate, I'm doing the same thing with the one bit of privilege I got — which is my music. The difference is my privilege is God-given."

The food came and we spoke more about *Half Price Wings*. There were six songs on it, and one of them was called "8-Bit Dream," which he'd performed earlier. He said this was going to be the one that made him. It was doing well on streaming services and had gotten played on some underground music shows. He told me he'd been invited to do a three-song performance on an up-and-coming YouTube show that showed off new talent.

That was when labels would be interested, he said. That's when the money, the crew, and the future would come.

"What if you're not happy when you get all that stuff?" I asked between bites.

"I'd rather be unhappy and rich than unhappy and broke."

"Careful what you wish for though, right? That's all I'm saying."

Halo looked up from his mountain of pancakes and I sensed he was about to launch into a tirade at me — his calm seemed shaken. We were interrupted by a kid. I say kid, he was probably about twenty. He slowly approached the table, his hands pressed together.

"Hey, sorry, you're Halo, right?"

Halo glanced up to him and his calm was back again — any anger I'd awoken had subsided.

"That's me, man."

Halo wiped his mouth with his hand and shuffled out of the booth before the kid had even asked for anything.

"You want a selfie?" Halo asked. "Go ahead. Hey, better yet — this guy can take it. Yo, take a photo of us."

I put down my fork and the kid handed me his phone. I got out of the booth as the kid mumbled something nervously about "8-Bit Dream."

The kid smiled at the camera and Halo held his head high — one hand on the brim of his baseball cap, the other on the kid's shoulder.

I handed the kid his phone back and he walked away. We sat back in the booth.

"That kid right there," Halo said. "He watches each one of my YouTube videos, downloads each of my songs, and buys one ticket to one show — that's about a hundred bucks a year I'm making from him. I just need a million more kids like that and I've done it."

"A million more selfies?" I asked.

"Yeah," he laughed and coughed, spitting out bits of pancake. "A million more selfies. I like that."

The Heatwave - June 2022

We went to a comedy club last night because it was too hot to stay at home or sit outside. The heatwave had messed up the city — there had been a power cut in Echo Park, brownouts in Silver Lake, small wildfires igniting around the hills. The freeway had a rust-colored haze and everybody seemed hot, bothered, a little more intense.

The comedian was fine. He was engaging, had good timing, and a funny bit about when he drank ayahuasca with his wholesome mom in Peru.

"So I'm vomiting violently, crying, seeing God — you know, a typical Tuesday. Even the shaman is like, 'Holy shit, this guy is fucked up.'

My mom, meanwhile, she comes out of it like, 'Sweetheart, I just met your grandmother in the spirit realm. She gave me her gingersnap recipe.'

I'm like, that's cool, Mom. I'm over here trying not to shit my soul out, and I just saw Satan climbing up my leg with a knife in his teeth, but I'm happy for you."

The only thing I found off-putting was that he had this weird way of holding the mic — his wrist was at a strange angle, like he was too cool to just speak into it. He had to have it hovering near the side of his face, turning his head to talk.

A drunk guy in the back of the room started heckling him at some point. It wasn't even that bad or insulting — it actually sounded like the guy was a fan.

"Sir, what are you talking about? You know nobody can hear you, right? That's why they don't hand mics to the crowd — it generally doesn't work at a comedy show. What's that? Ohhhhh, okay."

The comedian shrugged at the rest of the crowd and pulled a face that said, *I still have no idea what he's trying to say.*

The guy didn't stop.

"Can I ask you a question? Please don't take any offense. But are you a slow kid or something? It's fine if you are. It actually explains a lot."

This made the heckler louder — maybe he felt like he was now part of the show — but he didn't stop.

The comedian's face changed, dropping what everyone could now see had been an act up until that point. He held the mic firmly to his lips like a politician in a town hall.

"You know what? You're screwing up my flow. All the people here tonight have paid to watch a comedy show, and you're messing it up for them all. I'm not an asshole — I'm really not — but doing this… look, I work really hard on it. There's a rhythm that has to go with it. It's my art, man, you know, and you're screwing with it."

To his credit, he tried to shift the topic, tried a few more lines, but none of them landed. The audience was distracted now. The sweat on his forehead shone under the spotlight, and one of his eyes was twitching — that nervous blink thing some people do.

The heckler started back up again, and the comedian stood looking at him like he might start crying. With a swing of his arm, he threw the microphone into the crowd like a baseball pitcher. I'm sure he was meaning to hit the heckler, but he missed and hit a woman two seats over in the nose.

The crowd gasped as the sound system spat out a screech of feedback. The comedian immediately grimaced, closing his fists to his face as he watched the mic bounce off the woman's face. The heckler seemed completely unaware of any of this, shouting,

"Do the bit about your cat!"

The comedian vanished into the wings, and people waited to see if he was coming back or whether this whole thing was a bit. The woman had people pressing napkins to her bleeding nose now — so if it was a bit, it was a really good bit.

Then someone booed. Then there were more boos. Eventually the whole room was booing at the empty stage.

Outside, there was still a relentless heat. The night now smelled of food, tar, exhaust, and weed. We got into our Uber and drove east on Sunset with all the windows down. The city felt like it was being fired in a kiln. The driver had an energy drink in the console and kept wiping his brow with the palm of his hand. Scoot Brewer was on the radio talking politics and saying the country was losing its way in all areas (his guy was no longer president).

At stoplights, the world came into little frames. A couple fought next to a wall with a mural of a giant ice cream cone with eyes. Two influencers filmed each other dancing by a bus bench. A man sold roses from a milk crate to the traffic — not selling one.

At a 7-Eleven, the car stopped and the driver tapped the wheel to the rhythm of the talk radio. Scoot had angered someone, and they were shouting at him now. On the sidewalk, a homeless guy crouched in an attack stance, barefoot, eyes wide. Three security guards in black stepped toward him but kept their distance. The man pivoted, performed a pretty impressive roundhouse kick that didn't connect with anything. One guard caught his ankle midair just as the light changed and we rolled on.

We climbed into Beachwood Canyon at one in the morning — traffic was still heavy, and there were people walking dogs on the small patches of grass around the streets. The Hollywood sign was somewhere ahead, invisible, lost in the darkness of the hills.

The Uber dropped me near the top. The driver wished me luck getting to sleep.

The porch boards were warm, even under my shoes. From up here, L.A. looked like it had been pieced together out of tiny dots of light — thousands of white lights in distant windows, the blinking lights of planes dropping over the black outline of the city, red lights across the tops of unseen skyscrapers.

There was no sleeping tonight, I was pretty certain. I took a bottle of water from the fridge, turned the air-con on, and lay on the sofa reading a book. The neighbor's dog was barking relentlessly. Then a helicopter buzzing low over my roof. I stopped reading after two pages and put music on instead.

I lay there — my body warm, uncomfortable — and controlled my breathing, focusing on the music, trying to ignore the heat.

Then the dream started again. It had been a recurring dream that I'd had for twenty or so years. Not every night, but every now and again.

I was barefoot, the stone floor cool under my feet. It was a small church with white plastered walls. It was bright. Like, so bright. There was a window with no glass in it about nine feet above the floor, and you could only see a beautiful blue sky through it. It felt like we were in the Mediterranean. There were no pews in the church, just old wooden chairs, most of them mismatched.

The church was always empty, and I was always sitting in the middle. There was no crucifix, no Jesus — just empty chairs facing forward to an empty space. I was always filled with absolute peace, absolute calm. I could only hear my own breathing and the soft hum of the world outside — a breeze, trees moving, birds singing.

Nothing ever happened in the dream. It was just that. Like I was waiting to meet someone there — or someone was going to meet me there.

Salvation was on the way in some form, and this was an idyllic place to wait it out.

When I awoke, I woke like a man who had just been saved from drowning. One of my earphones had fallen out, and I was gasping for breath in the dry air.

I checked my phone — it was 5:30 a.m.

The sun was just starting to burn through the sky. L.A. was no longer lights but now faint, unsure shapes of buildings in the haze.

I stepped out onto the terrace and was hit with a cool morning air that promised renewal. My mind was wide awake but my body was tired. A fire truck wailed somewhere nearby.

I stood there barefoot, the wooden decking cool now, and for a moment I could almost feel the church from the dream — the quiet, the blue sky through the window.

The heat would come back. It always did.

But for now, there was something cooler in the air.

Halo Part Two – July 2023

I got a DM from Halo in April. He was heading out on a world tour starting at some festival in Northern California in May, hitting Europe in July and August before going to Asia and Australia next year. A hundred dates. He said he'd already sold half a million tickets.

I replied saying I'd love to see a show and asked how his mom was. He didn't respond, which wasn't a surprise. I hadn't seen Halo since two summers ago in Mid-Wilshire but had occasional DMs from him he never replied to. His messages were always brags dressed up as news about how he was doing. I didn't get why he felt he needed to prove something or show off — to me of all people — because everybody knew who Halo was now. *Half Price Wings* was huge. *A Million Selfies* had gone into the most-played lists of 2022.

His Insta posts were full of crowds, gold, cars, the Hollywood Hills, pool parties. He'd bought a tiger. He had his own tequila range. He'd spent last Christmas in Fiji, and it looked like he'd flown twenty people out with him on a private jet.

Ten weeks after that world-tour DM, I got another message — this time from his manager. He gave me ticket details and an invitation to his hotel, The ********** in London.

Say you have an appointment to see Mr. Goldmouth.

In the black cab on the way to the hotel, there was a giant billboard in Wandsworth with a shirtless Halo on stage, an all-black background and, in giant white letters:

HALF PRICE WINGS — THE WORLD TOUR.

Seeing Londoners, tourists, black cabs, and red buses pass underneath a giant picture of a guy I'd watched in the back of an art gallery felt surreal. It was two worlds colliding that were probably never intended to meet — and that's how I felt on my way to the hotel.

I'm not interested in all this excess stuff, am I? I like rap. I like musicians. But the materialism and the gold and everything else didn't do anything for me. That's all Halo seemed to be about now, from what I could see.

From the cab window I watched planes dropping into London and pictured one of them being Halo's private jet. A stranger from a strange land, dropping in, grabbing everything he could carry, and taking off again for sunnier shores.

The doorman, dressed in coat tails and a top hat, opened the cab door. I thanked him and walked inside the lobby. I'd never been in The ********** before — I had no business ever being in The **********. Everything seemed to be either mahogany, marble, or gold.

I hate this. I snuck a photo on my phone of the giant golden mirror on the wall.

The woman at the front desk looked like a model, her hair and makeup done like she was about to go on stage.

"I'm here to see Mr. Goldmouth?" I mumbled, embarrassed.

"Excuse me?" she asked, leaning forward.

"I'm here to see Mr. Goldmouth."

"I'm sorry, sir, can you speak up?"

"I'M HERE TO SEE MR. GOLDMOUTH."

Other eyes in the lobby looked over at me.

"Ah yes, we're expecting you. Paulo will show you up to his suite."

I nodded a thank-you and Paulo spawned in from nowhere — pale, polite, dressed in a suit like the desk clerk. His steps made no sound, like he was walking on the balls of his feet.

"Do you have any cases, sir?" he asked.

"No."

"Wonderful. Right this way."

Paulo took me up in the elevator to the top floor.

The floor was alive when we stepped out. First the smell — a mix of weed, fried food, cologne, and something else I couldn't place. Halo's security — two giant guys — stood on opposite ends of the corridor, both in black T-shirts and gray suits a size too big.

Double doors in the middle of the corridor flung open and there he was — Halo, robe half open, giant boxers with printed lips, the same chain, heavy as ever, around his neck. Two women in short skirts and bras sat on the couch. Various guys were around the room, maybe twelve. Some working — locked into phone calls or laptop screens. Others lounging and smoking. More guards planted in the corners like statues. A basketball game played on mute across a TV the size of a wall, and music boomed from one of the bedrooms. It was Halo's music.

This was Halo's court, and Halo was king.

"My boy!" Halo bellowed, as if we'd spoken yesterday. He laughed wheezily, grabbed my hand, and pulled me in for half a hug.

"My guy," he said. "You see this?"

He walked over to the giant windows that looked out at the Thames and a cloudy London. I smiled and said I'd seen his billboard on the way to the hotel.

Halo grinned wider.

"They love me here, man. We're taking over the whole city this week."

He offered me a drink; I said no. He poured a glass of champagne and handed it to me anyway.

For a while it was small talk, half-shouted over his music. Stories about Fiji, the jet, about how many streams *A Million Selfies* was on now (approaching a billion). Every sentence had a number in it — whether a sale or a dollar amount. Every laugh stayed open a fraction too long, flashing gold teeth.

Halo sat beside the girls, stroking the leg of one of them. His other arm rested on the back of the sofa, his robe fully open now. I perched on the edge of an armchair, politely sipping the champagne I'd been given.

"Where's that fucking kid with the chemicals?" Halo boomed. One of the guys took this as his cue to stand up and hurry out of the suite.

At some point I realized I didn't like Halo. Maybe jealousy. Maybe I was just tired of the bragging. Either way, I couldn't help myself. One of my failings is it's always been hard for me to pretend I'm happy being somewhere I don't want to be or in the company of someone whose company I don't want. My natural response is to fuck things up.

"How's your mom doing? You were living with her this time last year, right?" I said. The girls pulled a face like they'd just learned something astounding and looked at Halo.

Halo's expression didn't change, but darkness seemed to pull in around his edges.

"Mom's fine," he said.

"Cool," I nodded and sipped my champagne. "You take her to Fiji with you for Christmas?"

"Nah. She stayed at my aunt's. She don't like flying."

I nodded.

Halo started drumming the back of the sofa with his fingers. He wasn't stroking the girl's leg anymore. He looked around at nothing, sniffed, pinched his nose.

"Hey, you remember me telling you I was gonna do all this?" Halo said. "And you asked me if it would be enough? I got your answer for you."

He grinned, flashing gold.

"You've done really well. Seriously, congratulations," I said. "My only point was doing things for the right reason. Remember being in the restaurant and seeing the words on the wall that became the title of your EP — like it was meant to happen? Moments like that are golden — more golden than all of this. If you keep making stuff, then you're a success, right?"

"I'm a success," Halo said.

"I didn't say you're not," I laughed awkwardly and took another sip of champagne.

"You're sayin' I sold out."

"I'm not saying… ah, fuck it, I don't know what I'm saying."

"You're saying I'm a sell-out and my success isn't really success. Well, I don't see you complaining, sitting here in this hotel drinking my champagne."

"You invited me here. You poured the champagne despite me saying I didn't want a drink."

"Keep talking," Halo said, repositioning himself to the edge of the couch, hands clasped.

"What did I say?"

"You're saying enough, motherfucker. I knew I didn't like you when we met in L.A. You're some fucking hater or something."

"I'm not a hater. It's just I can only take someone mentioning their net worth so many times in a single conversation before it starts to feel like a drag. I like you! You had talent!"

"HAD!? HAD!?" Halo rose to his feet, shouting.

All the eyes in the room were on us now. The music kept thudding.

"Not had — I didn't mean that — I meant… I don't know. I'm happy for you. You got exactly what you want."

I wasn't being sarcastic and I was actually trying to calm the fire I'd started, only it didn't work. The next thing I knew, Halo's giant hands grabbed my shirt and he dragged me out of the chair. The coffee table flipped — glasses, champagne, and food went flying. The girls screamed and moved.

Halo threw me into a side table that snapped under my back. I didn't think — it all happened suddenly. It seemed, in that second, the best thing to do was pick up one of the giant lamps and hurl it at Halo. He put his arm up to block it, but it smashed and caught some of his head all the same. Bits of the lamp flew in all directions, smashing a mirror and more glasses.

"FUCKER!" Halo shouted and stomped toward me.

I'd barely got back to my feet when he lunged, like a rugby tackle. We crashed over the sofa, tipping it backward, and staggered into the dining table — more glass shattering, drinks flying. Some of the guys grabbed their laptops and ducked out of the way.

I swung back at Halo, mostly to keep him off me, and suddenly we were wrestling, shoving, rolling on the floor — two idiots tearing at each other on the patterned carpet. His giant hand pushed against my face as he hit me in the ribs. I used both hands to push his face away from mine.

The guards stood watching, blank-faced, like this wasn't the first time they'd seen Halo fighting and were just waiting for the right moment to intervene.

"DON'T!" Halo barked between grunts. "DON'T TOUCH HIM!"

I managed to knee him in the balls and he made a sound like he'd burned himself on a hot pan. He grabbed his crotch, got to his feet, and staggered backward. He tripped over an overturned chair and crashed down against the room-service trolley. Metal went flying.

Finally, we stopped. Both panting. Shirts twisted, faces marked red, cheeks flushed. The room was wrecked around us. He was propped on one elbow on the floor, one hand still cupping his crotch.

"See?" he said, voice low, still panting. "I won. I got everything, and what do you have? You don't got nothing."

I left the hotel and didn't go to the show.

Weeks later I read the headline when I woke up: Halo drowned in his pool in the Hills during a tour break. Nobody knew if it was by accident or not. There were videos on news sites of candles lined up outside the gates, kids crying, holding up merch. #RIPHalo trended for six days straight.

I think of him shirtless under that palm tree in L.A. I think of him in London, his stupid alias at the hotel desk, dragging me down with him into the penthouse carpet. And I think of the last thing he said to me:

I got everything and what do you have? You don't got nothing.

He was right — but not in the way he meant.

We still follow each other on Insta.

A Gentle Rebellion - August 2024

Everything is awful, of course.

During a press conference in the garden of 10 Downing Street, Prime Minister Sir Keir Starmer stood behind his podium in the August London sunshine, looked right at you, and said:

"Things are worse than we ever imagined."

It wasn't exactly Barack Obama's "Yes We Can" speech.

Keir had sat the nation down opposite him at the kitchen table, held its hand, looked it in the eye, and told it:

"Honey, we've lost all our money in some kind of crypto scam. We have to sell the house and move in with my mother."

The British response wasn't shock or anger. It was simply, *"Oh, okay, let me go pack."*

Because we've been through this before — numerous times. Being British and paying tax is like living with a compulsive gambler. You and I keep making money, we're quite sensible with it, but for some reason we're always short, and our other half needs more.

It was Gordon Brown selling our gold for just one more bet. It was a variety of Conservative leaders selling the NHS for just a little bit more of a taste. And now it's Sir Keir's turn to root through the tin of money you hide in your sock drawer and sell your TV to "fix the economy."

So what do we do?

Well, not much.

Because it's all very uninteresting, and we have zero control over any of it.

So we just know we need a job of some kind. We need income — the more, the better. It's nice if you enjoy the job, but not crucial.

The idea of keeping a job, not out of freedom of choice but because it's necessary, is nothing new.

In the '90s, counterculture fought hard against the 9-to-5. Movies like *Office Space* and *Fight Club* showed Generation X trapped in fluorescent-lit prisons, rebelling against a life that went against every primeval instinct.

Millennials took it further. We're not locked into gray cubicles anymore. Many of us work from home or in offices that try to be adult daycares. Want a super-comfy chair? No problem. Want extra breaks away from your screen? Absolutely. We've managed to make work and workplaces, by and large, quite comfortable.

But we're still there because we *have* to be there. And our answer to that has been the rise of *quiet quitting*.

It's a brilliant act of passive rebellion. We couldn't actually quit, because we need the paycheck and the job's comfortable, but we don't want it to define our lives.

You're still there, technically, but your spirit has floated gently out the window. For every piece of actual work you complete, you do some online shopping. You stretch your lunch break. You make sure you stand up from your computer and walk around every hour. You chat with coworkers, sloping around like you're killing time in a café.

And before you know it, it's time to go home. You've done the bare minimum, lived your life, stayed awake through the afternoon, ignored work on the weekends, and then picked up your paycheck at the end of the month.

It's like being paid to attend a dreary dinner party. You try to enjoy it, you make polite conversation, and at the first acceptable moment — you leave.

Let's take a moment to appreciate the audacity of this new way of working. Quiet quitting is the passive-aggressive way of saying:

"I've had enough of pretending to care about your interminable meetings and your motivational posters featuring cats hanging off branches."

Quiet quitting tells your company:

"I know my worth. I know what my time is worth. Me just being here and doing exactly what I need to do is enough. Any extra energy is reserved for me and the things I care about."

For boomers, the workplace was a temple of grind-it-out capitalism, where staying late, burning out, and sacrificing your family were badges of honor.

"Burnout" itself was coined when the inevitable happened — when those overachievers finally realized this way of living wasn't sustainable, that there had to be more to life than work.

So alongside "burnout," millennials created a new mantra:

"I'm not paid to care."

If an invite says *optional*, you're not going. If it says *mandatory*, you'll go — but that's all you'll do.

Of course, the corporate world is in full damage-control mode. "Engagement seminars!" they cry. "Team bonding!" Anything to drag us back into the cult of the workplace.

But what they haven't figured out is that these old tricks don't work anymore. No seminar or away day will ever be more engaging than scrolling your Instagram feed for things that actually interest you.

Some say it's a survival mechanism — a way to navigate the exhausting grind of week after week, year after year. But it feels like more than that. It's a counterculture — one that's practical, realistic, and rooted in the simple truth that we still need to pay rent.

We've made a truce with ourselves — a collective shrug toward ambition — and redefined productivity into something more palatable:

"I'm here, aren't I?"

So here we sit in our office chairs, scrolling social media, devoting time to our side hustles, waging a quiet siege of comfort over the chaos of the world.

It's about embracing mediocrity in the one part of life that deserves to be mediocre — work — and saving our energy for the parts that truly matter.

So, as Sir Keir Starmer tells us the economy is now on palliative care, *quiet quitting* has become the ultimate rebellious act.

While we've long been told that dedication is the pathway to success, it turns out that stepping back is the pathway to peace.

Magdalena – July 2024

Magdalena sat naked at her dresser, wiping makeup from her face with slow, deliberate strokes. Her hair spilled over one shoulder — black, the kind of black that swallows light; the kind of black that one artist tried to copyright once. I forget his name.

The room smelled faintly of jasmine — the scent of someone who's been expensive for a long time. A single lamp glowed gold against the mirror; everything outside its reach faded into shadow.

She caught my eyes in the reflection and studied me lying in the giant white duvet on the bed.

"You have two different colored eyes," she said.

"Do I?"

"One's greener, the other one blue."

Her tone carried no curiosity, only quiet amusement — as if she were appraising a painting she didn't intend to buy. No sense that she was telling someone what their own eye color was, as if they weren't already aware.

"That's cool," she murmured, dabbing beneath her jawline. "Do you think they'll ever let you change your eye color with surgery in the future?"

"You probably already can."

She shrugged, dismissing both my response and me.

"I'm *au naturel*," she said, then smiled faintly. "Except my nose. This isn't the nose I was born with."

She set the cotton ball down, rearranged a few bottles into perfect symmetry, then opened a small metal jewelry box beside the mirror. From it she drew a clear plastic baggie, the powder inside faintly pearlescent under the lamplight. She dipped a fingernail in and brought it to her nose. One clean inhale — eyes closed, lips slightly parted.

"You want?" she asked, looking at me in the mirror again. Her voice was casual, generous in a way that wasn't really generous.

"That's alright."

A faint smile touched her lips.

"You're on your best behavior," she said, resealing the bag. She slipped it back into the box and shut the lid with a quiet metallic click.

The bedroom was larger than an entire floor of my house. The carpet was so thick it swallowed sound. At the far end, tall white doors waited. She crossed the room barefoot and pushed them open.

Warm air drifted in, carrying the sound of crickets and the faint trickle of a fountain. Somewhere below, the lights of her swimming pool illuminated the chemical turquoise. Beyond the garden, the dark slope of Beverly Hills spread out like a soundstage — palms, quiet roads, distant sirens. A police helicopter drifted low across the canyon, its searchlight sweeping briefly over the ridge before vanishing again.

We'd met a few weeks earlier at an art show downtown. She was a name — one of those collectors who appear in photographs standing just close enough to the artist to suggest possession. In photographs, she never smiled, and one foot was always turned in and behind her other leg.

That night she'd bought a $25,000 statue of a fish — chrome and grotesque, the size of a car — and they'd delivered it earlier that day, lowering it into her garden with a crane. They broke an urn or a plant pot or something, and she was super pissed and screamed at the delivery guys for like ten minutes straight.

She leaned on the doorframe, watching the lights ripple in the pool.

"I hate that fucking fish now," she said, sighing, staring out into the dark.

"So why buy it?" I asked.

She turned slightly, pearls at her throat catching the lamplight.

"Oh, sweet dumb boy," she said, "that's why you're an artist and not an art collector."

She walked back toward me, unhurried. She stopped in front of me, close enough for her perfume to catch my nose. She brushed a strand of hair from my face and patted my head in a gesture that was half affection, half ownership.

"How much was the Saville?" I asked, pretending to keep it casual. *Nude With Joyous Painting* had hung over the bed and overlooked us having sex numerous times over the weeks. I'd Googled to see whether it could be the original, and there was a possibility, but I didn't dare ask.

She smiled.

She climbed onto the bed — one knee, then the other, pressing into the sheets. The mattress dipped beneath her weight as she rose, balancing in two slow steps until she stood above me, her naked body towering, a foot planted on either side of my body.

The lamplight traced the line of her bare skin, the curve of her hip, the glint of pearls resting just above her breasts. For a moment she seemed perfectly balanced, composed — a sculpture caught between movement and stillness.

"I like you," she said softly. "But we don't know each other well enough to talk about money."

Magdalena texted me at 3 a.m. one Wednesday morning when I was in my own bed.

Throwing a party at the gallery. Going to reveal your portrait of me. 8 p.m. Friday. Wear something smart, don't be too artisty now. xoxox

I lay there staring at the message, half asleep, half waiting for it to vanish.

She had asked me to paint her a couple of weeks before, and I had. I painted, as I usually did, just from memory. When I finished it, I offered to bring it over to her place to show her, but she said no. She said she wanted it to be a reveal — a surprise. She said it was the perfect reason to throw a party and for her friends to see it at the same time she did.

The painting was now wrapped in brown paper and cardboard, leaning against the wall by my front door.

Her gallery was near Marina del Rey, a flat black façade with *Magdalena Martin* painted in gold letters across the top of the door. By the time I arrived, the street outside was already full — cars parked bumper to bumper and others circling, looking for spaces.

The gallery doors stood open, spilling light and the sound of a crowd into the warm night.

Inside, there were very few paintings on the walls and too many people. For every painting, there were probably twenty people. Bodies pressed together in expensive fabrics — perfume, cologne, champagne, glasses, and the hum of many small conversations happening at once. None of them conversations at all — just alternating monologues of self.

At the back of the gallery, the courtyard glowed under strings of exposed light bulbs.

Magdalena caught my eye and moved through the crowd with ease. The navy dress, its straps around her arms, her signature black hair over one shoulder — always the same shoulder — the diamond-encrusted watch, the diamond bracelet, the diamond necklace, all flickering and shining under the light. She was a constellation.

"The fucking DJ is late," she said in a low whisper when she got close to me. "I'm going to pour my champagne over his decks and electrocute the motherfucker if he doesn't get here soon." She then smiled and waved, her eyes catching someone across the room.

Her eyes were darting everywhere, locking onto ten different things in ten different milliseconds.

She gestured toward the parcel in my hands.

"It goes on the easel in the courtyard. Michael will handle it."

Michael ran the gallery and manned it like a lone soldier the four days a week it opened. He was middle-aged, wore green spectacles, and a bow tie with his suit. He appeared from behind Magdalena, collected the parcel without saying anything, and disappeared back into the crowd.

I stayed in one place, unsure whether to move. The gray suit I'd bought on discount earlier that day was probably a size too small — uncomfortable and scratchy. I tried to make subtle movements to stretch out the fabric in places it was pulling.

The gallery was still filling up. The temperature shifted with each new group of people that arrived — screams, cries of greeting, another gust of perfume, another roar of laughter.

There was no food, I noticed, just a long table with a black cloth and rows of champagne and flutes.

Magdalena floated from group to group, completely unphased — linking into different groups, instantly placing herself at the center of whichever conversation she entered. Her posture, her jawline, her sharp cheekbones. And her eyes.

Jesus Christ.

Oh no.

No.

Fuck, fuck, fuck.

Fuck me, no.

She had brown eyes.

The thought landed in my mind with the velocity of a bullet.

Why did I think they were green? I'd painted them green. Not even a soft green, but a bright, loud green — the kind a clown would use to paint his eyebrows.

The room suddenly felt even more packed, the sound all the more overwhelming.

Sweat was dripping down my back under the layers of T-shirt and suit jacket.

I looked through the crowd toward the courtyard. The easel sat in the middle of everyone, now covered — a purple silk sheet draped over it like a body in the morgue.

The DJ arrived, a Black French guy called Omar with dreadlocks and a denim jacket. He sloped in with a laptop in one hand and a rucksack in the other, plugging things into the speakers and decks that sat on a stand on one side of the gallery.

My heart had started to race.

I thought about bouncing but thought against it. I considered going to collect myself in the restroom — a single toilet down a spiral staircase to the basement. The problem was the restroom was no longer a restroom; it was the cocaine room tonight, and people were streaming down there in pairs.

Would she mind I got her eyes wrong? Would it even be noticeable?

I looked over at Magdalena, who was giving a death stare to the DJ from across the room.

Bass kicked into the air and EDM started playing.

"What do you see?" a woman asked me.

"Sorry?"

"I saw you looking at the painting on the wall. What do you see?"

She gestured toward a piece that was abstract — perfect shapes, perfectly meaningless.

I hadn't actually looked at it but had stared through it, running through all the ways I might avoid the portrait reveal, or how I could just disappear. LAX wasn't far away. Twenty hours from now, I could be in Greece.

"I think the rectangle is water," I said. "The circles above it are lights or something. I don't know."

"Well," the woman smiled, "if that's what you see, that's what you see."

She disappeared back into another group, another conversation, and I was swallowed by another swell of people.

The guests were multiplying. A movie producer bragged about a documentary he was working on. A writer said streaming companies were circling his unpublished novel. An actress said I'd probably seen her in a TV show that summer.

Someone said, *"I'm on a fast — this is my fourth day. I'm trying to extract salt from my body."* Another person said, *"Let me stand here so I can conversate with you guys."*

I'd never heard that word before and wasn't sure it was a word.

"L.A. is over now," someone else said to me. "I'm buying a place in Texas."

Everybody was friendly. I found most people in L.A. friendly. But nobody asked me what I did. I found most people in L.A. didn't ask what I did.

Magdalena appeared beside me again, escorting a woman holding a small Yorkshire Terrier.

"This is Milan," Magdalena said, and I was unsure whether she meant the woman or the terrier.

It bared its teeth and snarled at me.

"He's friendly, darling. He won't bite," the woman said.

"This is the boy I was telling you about," Magdalena said. "Say hello."

"Hi," I said.

At thirty-seven, I didn't feel like a boy.

"Look at his eyes," Magdalena said, "one blue, one green."

"Oh, how horrendous for you," the woman said, clutching her dog.

A man nearby asked if I could see differently out of them. I didn't answer. I excused myself toward the open doors, pretending I'd seen someone else I wanted to talk to.

By eight-thirty, Marina del Rey glittered in layered blues. The music grew louder and Omar tapped at his laptop, hopping from one foot to the other. The crowd began to gravitate toward the courtyard — anticipation thick in the air.

The music stopped. Magdalena took her position at one side of the easel; Michael stood at the other.

Somewhere deep in my brain, a voice repeated: *green eyes, brown eyes, green eyes, brown eyes.*

Magdalena said a few words I didn't hear. She gestured to me, and there was applause.

Michael turned and pulled back the silk.

There was a hush — the hush of a murder trial before the verdict.

The portrait shone in the low light: Magdalena.

And the eyes.

The bright, green eyes.

Milan growled something in dog from somewhere unseen behind me.

I waited for it — the correction, the explosion, the humiliation.

Instead came applause — polite, rhythmic. The expensive sound of expensive people pretending to like something.

Magdalena didn't clap. She stepped toward the painting, studied it the way you'd study your reflection in a window at night. She looked into her own eyes for a long moment, then smiled — a small curl of a smile, a smile of genuine satisfaction.

"Perfect," she said.

A conveyor belt of faces passed by me, saying things like:

"Such clever choices."
"Stunning use of color."
"Looks just like her."

By 11 p.m., the party began to subside.

"I'm gonna go," I said to Magdalena, managing to grab her attention for the first time since the reveal.

"Michael is driving me home soon. You don't want to come back with me?" she said and kissed me, holding my waist.

"You should enjoy the rest of your party. I'm good for nothing but my bed right now."

"Hmmm," she said and kissed me again. "I won't take it personally. Thank you for my portrait."

I didn't hear from Magdalena for a few days after that. I texted her a couple of times, asked if she wanted to meet for dinner, but she didn't respond.

I sat around my house. I painted, I wrote, I checked my phone, watched TV, checked my phone again.

I went on her gallery website to see if there were photos from the party — there weren't. I clicked through the artwork she had for sale and came across one staring back at me from the screen.

Magdalena — $500.

It was my portrait of her. It was also the cheapest fucking painting in the gallery.

I called an Uber and reached Magdalena's house thirty minutes later. Her giant gates were closed, so I pushed the intercom that sat below a small camera on the wall.

There was no response, but I could hear the clicking of sandals coming down the driveway behind the gates.

The door to the side opened slightly and Magdalena stood in her robe, looking around it.

"What the fuck?" I said.

"Yeah, look, I've been busy."

"Not about not responding. I'm talking about the portrait — you're selling it for $500 on your website!?"

"Oh, that? Well, yeah. I'm an art dealer, sweetheart. I deal in art."

"I thought it was just for you?"

She looked at me blankly.

"Did you even realize yet that I got your eyes the wrong cclor!?" I shouted.

Her expression didn't change.

"You did?" she said.

"Who is it?" a voice called from the house behind her — French accent.

I looked through the crack in the door and saw Omar, the DJ, step out wearing only tight white CK briefs.

"You fucked the DJ?" I shouted.

"Hey, man, fuck you," his voice came again, but I could no longer see him — Magdalena had closed the door to just a crack.

"Look, darling, don't be hurt. We were having fun and we had all we could," she said. "The best artists never stay in one place, remember that?.You shouldn't tie yourself down to anything or anyone."

She closed the door, and I was left standing on a palm-lined street in Beverly Hills, alone.

I looked up and down the street as if I was going to find an answer about what to do now.

I stomped some flowers by her gates and set off walking away.

It seemed like a suitable goodbye.

Self Portrait - December 2024

I never saw myself getting past forty, but we'll see.

That isn't meant to be morbid. It's just the way I've always thought about time — you're there, and then you're gone.

It's the same as my relationship with God. You're there, and then you're gone.

When I was in my twenties, I had a kind of revelation — a powerful, sudden realization as I lay in a hammock beneath a blue sky — that everything was fine.

God was in the sunshine, in the coincidences that happen throughout life, in the ugly times and the beautiful times.

I've found that when I open myself to that, when I appreciate the beauty in the world (and the ugliness), I get what I need from it. I get an understanding of my place in the world, and I get led to where I need to be.

I've messed this up sometimes — placing too much faith in the universe to take me where I need to be, letting it all rest on the flow of things when there were choices and changes I could have made.

I can't hide how I feel most of the time. It shows up in my face, in my voice, in how I go quiet when something hits a nerve.

A character flaw is that I'm sensitive — but only about people or things that mean a lot to me. Most people and things don't. That sounds cold, but I'm not a cold person. I'm warm and loving. But you can't love everything.

I shouldn't be so dismissive. I should give people opportunities. I should be more empathetic. I tell myself that.

I want to be kind — I am kind — but others have made me feel I've been selfish, and sometimes I think, *fuck it, I'll do it that way then.*

It never lasts. I'll usually overcompensate afterward and give more of myself (or more of my money).

I've always done okay with money. It's always come along easily, but I'm indifferent toward it.

I've always been well paid, even as a kid. I live comfortably. I just need enough for books, records, streaming services, traveling, and Christmas. Nice hotel rooms and nice restaurants too. Nice things.

I like Christmas. I like Halloween. I love summer. I love New Year's Day but not New Year's Eve.

The worst month is January though — we can all agree on that.

I like slow mornings, long nights, lie-ins, sea air — anything sea-related.

I couldn't imagine not living near the sea. I'm very laid-back, but I get anxious when I'm waiting by myself.

I'm spontaneous to the point where I don't like to over-plan. I don't have a routine.

I'm a great traveler though — always organized and never have issues.

When it's too quiet, I don't like it.

I've learned I don't like being alone with myself that much, but I haven't found many people I like being with either.

It's kind of messed up. When I do find someone I enjoy being around, and they enjoy being around me, it's pure, honest, authentic. Divine.

I like cats and dogs; I'm both a cat and a dog person.

Kids are given a really bad deal in the world.

They have no money, little support, no say in how their world is run — and then they're told they're too loud, too feral, too detached.

They're told things were better before they were born.

You should hold your head high.

Do what you want to do, as long as it doesn't hurt anyone.

That's what I love about L.A. — everyone does their own thing and there's no judgment, just millions of people living their lives.

The U.K. is the opposite: a hive of people trying to remain within the hive, living their lives through other people's judgment.

You should skate in empty pools.

Experiment. Stay up all night. See sunrises. The nights are the best times of day.

I'm a night person but need the sunshine.

Read books. Read as many books as you can. Listen to music as much as you can.

Do whatever makes you happy and makes you feel like yourself.

Learn to stop doing things that make you unhappy.

Learn to say no.

I hate people who say "say yes to everything." Fuck that.

Be yourself. That's what you're good at.

Someone once told me you never know whose dog died that day, so be kind to everyone.

That being said, if someone tells me to do something, it's the quickest way to make sure I won't.

I'm not proud of it — it's some kind of block.

I like to find my own way, even if it's the long one.

I think I have misophonia, or whatever it's called.

Certain sounds set off an alarm in my head — cutlery scraping plates, the hum of a fridge, high-pitched electrical noises.

It's not anger; it's pain, but nowhere specific.

My brain just says, *We're being attacked.*

I live with it.

Pedro Almodóvar is one of my favorite writers. *Pain & Glory* is a masterpiece of storytelling — tender, self-aware, brave.

Julian Schnabel is another one of my favorites — his art, his filmmaking, his philosophy. He's a special kind of dude.

I don't want to create all the time — just for little bursts. I want to live my life too.

Art without truth isn't art at all, to me at least. But then again, art is what it is — whatever you create in that moment is art.

Most people don't understand art. Someone telling me art is good or bad is telling me they don't understand art.

I'd rather make one true thing than a hundred hollow things.

I'm happy with my life.

I've been to beautiful places, spent time with beautiful people, and had beautiful challenges.

I've created stuff that will outlive me.

I trust one person completely.

I've bonded with two people in my life and lost one of them.

I'm terrified of losing the other, but I think it'll be okay. I'm learning bonds stretch but never break.

I just want to be there, quietly, keeping on keeping on — a place of safety for them to come back to when they need anything.

I want to live loud, be vibrant, hurtling through it recklessly. I want to live in the sunshine, among the palms. I want to be a good dude. I want to buy a new hat.

They say to look at the wallpaper on someone's phone to know what they're most afraid to lose — and I've found this to be true.

Sometimes I wish I could be easier, simpler — the kind of person who's content without too much thought or questioning stuff.

I should stop confusing peace with boredom.

I don't know how useful any of this is.

Whatever it is you're doing — keep at it.

Do it well.

Life will take you along. If you try to control it, it just becomes an exercise in resistance and you won't get anywhere.

But other times, you can't just leave it all to the flow of things.

Sometimes you need to take action. You'll know it when the time comes.

Listen.

Breathe.

Appreciate the sunshine.

Follow your heart.

Have a good life.

I like you.

You'll be alright.

I think we'll be alright.

The Divine Ending - January 2025

The last time I was here — do you remember when — I'd like to go back.

Most of my thoughts the last couple of weeks started with one of those three.

Like when I opened the hotel room curtains and sunlight seeped in.

Do you remember when it was brighter, and warmer?

The Mediterranean was calm, rolling into the palm-lined beach.

The last time I was here there wasn't a path, just a track through the sand.

Children's voices and screams in the pool below are distant but loud.

I'd like to go back to England, but not in the wintertime.

It's still a fancy hotel; the staff still wear dark green waistcoats and bow ties.

There's a rule that if you come within ten feet of one of them, they have to greet you.

The ones about to clock off walk on the outskirts of the room.

"We remember you, sir — you were with your friend the last time you were here."

She's not here now. I don't miss her.

In the restaurant last night, one of the waiters slipped with a tray of drinks.

This was probably a mistake, of course.

You can't ever go back or relive something you had before.
All there was to do these last two weeks was walk the corridors —
the opulence, the gold, the chandeliers, the swan towels on the bed
every morning.

And I remember when.

I end up counting down the days to leaving.
I'm flying on the Thursday; my case is packed by the Monday.
Two weeks was enough — it was the New Year now.
I sit on the balcony on the last day, watching the playboys parasail.
There are new kids in the pool, just as loud, just as distant.
I'm in jeans and a hoodie despite the heat, ready for the plane.
I need to get to somewhere else.
It doesn't have to be perfect or special or whatever — just
somewhere else.

Do you remember the last time I was here?
I swear I saw lights dancing high above the horizon.

I splash water on my face right before I leave.
Paris first.
I'll spend a few days there.
Then back to California.

That's how all this ends anyway — with me meeting you there.

I might be a little late, but I'll meet you there.

ABOUT THE AUTHOR

CJ Story is a British born writer and artist.

He is also the author of;

Divine Anarchy: A Collection of Art & Writing
The Chaotic Last Days of Curtis Brown